Voyage into Mystery

Reports from the sinister side of the sea

I tell you naught for your comfort,
    Yea, naught for your desire,
Save that the sky grows darker yet
    And the sea rises higher.

Ballad of the White Horse
by G. K. Chesterton

Voyage into Mystery

Reports from the sinister side of the sea

RICHARD GARRETT

Weidenfeld and Nicolson – London

Published in Great Britain by
George Weidenfeld & Nicolson Limited
91 Clapham High Street
London SW4 7TA

This paperback edition published in 1991 by
George Weidenfeld & Nicolson Limited

ISBN 0 297 81106 1

Typeset at The Spartan Press Ltd,
Lymington, Hants

Printed in Great Britain by
The Guernsey Press Co. Ltd,
Guernsey, C.I.

Contents

Illustration Acknowledgements vi
Introduction 1

1. The Monstrous Ocean 4
2. Gone Missing 23
3. The Fire Bug 41
4. The Riddle of the *Gaul* 58
5. The Phantoms 74
6. Enigma Variations 91
7. Icebound 107
8. Crack Up 128
9. Ghost Story 142
10. Less than Innocent 158
11. The Ice Ship 173

Illustration Acknowledgements

The photographs in this book are reproduced by kind permission of the following:

Mary Evans Picture Library 1 above; *Malcolm Fussey* 4 above; *The Illustrated London News Picture Library* 3 below; *The Mansell Collection* 1 below; *Popperfoto* 3 above; *The Press Association* 2 below, 7 below; *Skyfotos* 7 above; *Syndication International* 2 above, 8 above.

Introduction

According to Longfellow:

> 'Wouldst thou' – so the helmsman answered –
> 'Learn the secret of the sea?
> Only those who brave its dangers
> Comprehend its mystery!'

One would like to think that these lines are true. I doubt, however, whether any thinking mariner would agree with them. Those whose business takes them across great waters obviously have a better understanding of the sea, but I doubt whether anyone is arrogant enough to suggest that he 'comprehends its mystery'. We are permitted, or so it seems to me, just so much knowledge and no more. If we were so completely informed, and if we acted wisely upon our knowledge, the number of lives forfeited each year to the ocean might diminish. Perhaps none would be lost at all.

As I remarked in my earlier book, *Flight into Mystery*, the greatest of all perplexities is Earth itself. What freak of chance or divine intent caused it to occur at the one place in our solar system in which life – intelligent life, life capable of creating wonderful things from the ingredients of the planet's composition – could thrive? This, surely, is the ultimate riddle, and everything else becomes small by comparison.

Edmund Burke, who could always be relied upon for a cogent remark, referred to 'the lucrative business of mystery'. There are many writers – of fiction and of non-fiction – who have found this to be true. Why, then, are we so absorbed by the unknown? Is it because our very lives are mysteries: that we really do not know why we exist, nor what our purpose is? Somebody – was it that crusty atheist Voltaire? I forget – suggested that, if there were no God, it would be necessary to invent one. If there is any truth in this, it must indicate an inherent desire to find a solution to the puzzle (anything beyond our understanding can be attributed to the Almighty). But, of course, it does not. It merely replaces one mystery with another.

There are many instances in which a carefully reasoned hypothesis will seem to provide an explanation. But, since there has been no material evidence to support them, such feats of the intellect would be unlikely to survive in a court of law. There are, again, cases that, for a while, were sufficiently mysterious – but which, in the end, were completely explained. So far as my own choice of subjects is concerned, these have qualified for admission into these pages. As I wrote in *Flight into Mystery*, a detective story is none the worse because it has a solution: readers would feel cheated without one.

If, then, we are in love with the apparently unexplained, we nonetheless look for an explanation. A cryptic crossword puzzle is an enigma. But it is there to be solved; anyone who attempts it (and fails) experiences a slight feeling of dissatisfaction. For that is another human attribute: curiosity.

Among the contents of these pages, you will find no more than one or two brief references to the *Mary Celeste*. I myself have written three accounts of the case and goodness knows how many other writers have involved themselves in it. It has already received more than enough coverage. You will find no mention of the *Rainbow Warrior*, the Greenpeace movement's flagship that was demolished in Auckland harbour by members of the French secret service. The case was solved so quickly and so completely, that there was really no mystery at all. I was tempted for a while to write about the liner *Queen Elizabeth*, which was burned to death at Hong Kong when being converted into a floating university. But there seemed to be too little evidence even for speculation.

I hope that my eventual selection may arouse your curiosity. Some of my subjects are more mysterious than others: a few hardly merit the description at all. But my motive, as always, has been simply to tell a good story: to entertain rather than to seek any higher truth.

Many people and many books have helped me to produce the present work. I should like to thank especially: Mr J. Kinahan of the National Union of Seamen, Mr R. A. Ridyard, Mr Fred G. Shaw, Lloyd's Shipping Information Services, the Department of Transport marine library, the librarians of the London Library, the National Maritime Museum, and the Imperial War Museum. Of the many newspapers and magazines I consulted, *Sea Breezes* and *Sea Classic International* were particularly helpful. Since this does not pretend to be a work of scholarship, I have assembled no bibliography though, among more recent sources, *Mysteries on the High Seas* by Philip MacDougall and *Into Thin Air* by Paul Begg were of the greatest help. I am also indebted to Miss Jane Blackett for her help and encouragement, and to Mrs Betty Jenner for her skill and patience at driving a typewriter.

Finally, to return to Longfellow, it may be that those who brave the sea's dangers are better qualified to comprehend its mystery – which does not mean to say that they are privy to all its secrets. On second thoughts, this, perhaps, is just as well. Complete knowledge might gratify our curiosity, but it might also make us complacent. We might begin to talk about 'conquering the ocean' – and meaning it. But the ocean would strike back. Carelessness would actually increase the number of casualties and we should be no better off. To borrow again from the admirable Burke, he certainly referred to 'The Great Instructor, Time,' but he also observed that 'The march of the human mind is slow.' As you may decide when you have read this book, it has not marched sufficiently quickly – even now in this age of advanced technology – to make us masters of the seas. Until, if ever, we are, there will continue to be mysteries.

Richard Garrett, Tunbridge Wells

I

The Monstrous Ocean

It is not, perhaps, easy to think of the ocean as a theatre: as an enormous stage upon which, from time to time, drama has taken place. Among its repertoire, like that of any other playhouse, are mysteries. But, if you will allow this rather far-fetched simile, the greatest mystery of all is how the theatre itself came to be created. It must either have been the result of divine purpose, or else a fluke beside which all other freaks of circumstance appear unremarkable.

Once upon a time, or so it is assumed, there was the Big Bang. It occurred between 10,000 million and 20,000 million years ago (in such an enormity of time, one is allowed to be vague). The bang was genesis – more or less. There was no Garden of Eden: no Adam tending nicely trimmed lawns, but an enormous explosion. Thus the universe was born. By no means the least of its mysteries is how, eventually, it arranged itself. Another question, of course, is what preceded it. Eternity stretches backwards as well as forwards. So what, one is bound to ask, existed before this explosion of all explosions? There is no answer.

The Earth was produced in a somewhat rudimentary form about 4,500 million years ago. It has become fairly well established that this is the only place – in our solar system, at any rate – capable of bearing life. The fledgling planet landed, if that is the correct word, in exactly the right place. It was neither too close to the sun (like Venus) nor too far away (like Mars). Not all that many miles out in one direction, its water would have evaporated in steam; in the other, it would have frozen solid and so it would have remained.

Mind you, the Earth was helped by the pull of its gravity. Without it, the water would have been slung off into space. So, too, would the atmosphere. End of story. No life; no oceans; nothing. Again, the margin of error was almost nil. Earth got it right.

Earth came in kit form that included all the essential components. For example, molten rock contains water. As the rocks cooled and hardened, the water vaporised and was absorbed into the atmosphere. Lower down, it was squeezed out and that, too, became vapour. One result of this was that the globe was covered by a thick canopy of cloud: so thick that the sun could not penetrate it. To say that it was dark may be wrong. But the light came from beneath; from the swirling red, orange, gold, super-heated, mass of matter that was the post-natal planet. Possibly the light was reflected off the cloud base. Perhaps there was light of a kind. But there was no sky to be seen.

Clouds produce rain. In this case, it seems to have been self-perpetuating. It fell on to the prodigiously hot rocks, was transformed into steam, and rose to rejoin the cloud mass from which it had escaped. This continued until the rocks had cooled down – a process that began when Earth had drifted far enough away from the sun. Then the water started to settle: in rivers, in lakes, and in enormous basins that were to become the oceans. As it, so to speak, came down from the hills, it brought with it sand and silt. Some ingredients – such as salt – were absorbed into it. The rest sank.

There used to be a theory that the moon was a chunk of matter which Earth, flamboyantly, had thrown into space. The very considerable cavity caused by its removal, once it was filled with water, became the Pacific Ocean. That was what they said. The Apollo missions, however, did a good deal to disprove this. The moon rocks contain more aluminium, calcium and magnesium than those of Earth – and less gold, bismuth and potassium. Oh yes – and more titanium. In any case, it has become generally accepted that the moon made its appearance at roughly, give or take a millenium or two, the same time as Earth. Thus, the astronomers suggested, it was either another planet that had been formed nearby – or else one that, wandering through the universe, had become trapped by Earth's gravity. Whatever the case, it has changed. About 3,500 million years ago, it was six times as large as it is now, one sixth of the present distance from Earth, and it shone thirty times more brightly than it does nowadays.

In the beginning – well, not quite the beginning, but the expression will have to serve – the land was neatly parcelled together in one mass and surrounded by the sea. There was nobody present to give it a name, but it is now known as Pangaea. One way of looking at it is by considering a designer. He roughs out an idea, studies it critically and decides that it will not do. And so he rubs it out and starts again. As the project advances, he modifies his concept again and again until, at last, he is satisfied. So it was with Earth. Pangaea contained all the components. It was a matter of arranging them correctly (whatever 'correctly' may mean in this context. There are so many secrets to which we are not privy). By about 100 million years ago, the so-called continental drift had split the original pack of land into two. In the north, there was Laurasia; in the south, Gondwanaland. But the process was not yet complete. The continents were still edging away from one another, until today's pattern was established. It was not unlike taking a jigsaw puzzle to pieces. For instance, a glance at a map of the world shows that the western coast of Africa would fit neatly into the eastern coast of South America. Furthermore, the rocks on each shore correspond in a way that cannot be attributed to coincidence. Another clue has been provided by the discovery of fossils in the Alps. Since they are of marine life, it must follow that these mountains were once beneath the sea.

The theory of 'continental drift' was first proposed by a German meteorologist named Alfred Wegener in the 1920s. This account of it is a considerable over-simplification, and it must be admitted that geologists found Herr Wegener's theories hard to believe. Later on, however, the prospect of continents actually being able to move provided such a neat solution to so many mysteries that Wegener's ideas came to be accepted.

But the original mystery remains. What act of God, or what freak of chance, positioned Earth so precisely between its neighbouring planets: the scalding chunk of hell that is Venus,

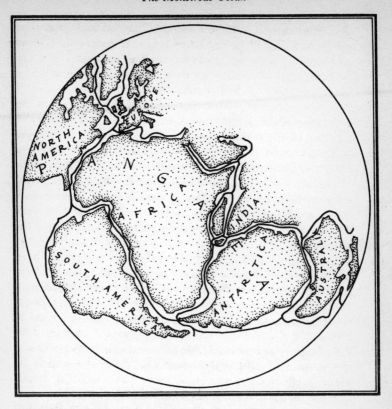

Map of the world about 100 million years ago, showing how the western coast of Africa would fit neatly into the eastern coast of South America.

and that frigid world, once so beloved by science fiction writers, that we call Mars? What, one asks oneself over and over again, was the purpose? Can one really accept the proposition that it was a fluke?

There are four elements: earth, water, air, and fire. It would be nice to add a fifth: life. But since, in one way or another, life depends on the Big Four, this may not be allowed. There is one school of thought that asserts that this unique property came from elsewhere in the universe. In a letter to *The Daily Telegraph* dated 1 December 1986, Professor Sir Fred Hoyle and Professor Chandra Wickramasinghe pointed out that: 'We have argued for several years that terrestrial life was seeded by microorganisms carried in comets and that bacteria and viruses are still being added to the Earth from outside.' Among them, if we are to believe these writers, is the AIDS virus. In this instance, the cause may have been 'a small comet disintegrating low in the atmosphere,' which could lead to 'pathogens [agents causing disease] being brought down in rainstorms that are geographically localised.'

So, according to this view, life and the source of its extinction by illness have the same – or very similar – origins. Two days later, on 3 December, Mr L. R. Croft, Lecturer in Biology at the University of Salford, gave his support to the Hoyle-Wickramasinghe hypothesis. Again in the *Telegraph* he remarked, 'Both these workers have recognised a fundamental flaw in the doctrine of evolution – namely the gigantic implausibility of the spontaneous formation of life on the primitive Earth.'

'The highly speculative "primeval soup" theory has been widely accepted largely because it is the only alternative to Biblical creationism.' 'Hoyle', wrote Mr Croft, 'has done a valuable service to science in bringing out into the open a problem about which there seemed to be a conspiracy not to discuss.'

Conspiracy or otherwise, the 'primeval soup' notion remains the favourite of most astronomers. Life, they believe, came as part of earth's package.

It originated in the sea: in shallow waters and in the form of cells that can, perhaps, be likened to algae. Initially each cell was self-sufficient. But, as time went by, they formed colonies, one linking up with another. Also, with the passage of time, a more sophisticated species developed. This was not self-sufficient: it fed off its more primitive neighbours. If we are to believe this, and if this was the origin of everything that lives – including man – it might be argued that here, in the very beginning, lies the clue to the subsequent behaviour of all living creatures. It might even be argued that poor old Adam and Eve should be absolved from Original Sin. It was the natural evolution of organic matter.

Nowadays, 70.8 per cent of the earth's surface is covered by oceans – 139,480,000 square miles. The mean depth is 2.20 miles – though, at its deepest (the Marianas Trench in the

Pacific), it descends to 6.58 miles. In other words, you could place Mount Everest into it and still have more than seven thousand feet to spare. However, the sea, too, has its highest mountain as well as its deepest depth. It was discovered in 1953 and lies close to the Tonga Trench between Samoa and New Zealand. The peak is 1,200 feet beneath the surface: the height, 28,500 feet above the seabed, is just short of Everest's 29,002 feet. Certainly if, by some horrific chance, the restraining powers of gravity were reduced, and the water was indeed spilt into space, a remarkable landscape would be revealed: rich in vegetation and as varied as that on land.

Inevitably, since curiosity is one of man's more praiseworthy characteristics, the ocean is the subject of more or less continual exploration. As recently as 1983 a new species of shark was discovered in the vicinity of Hawaii. It appears to be an undemanding creature living off a simple diet of plankton. It certainly cannot be described as a sea monster, which may be disappointing. Reports of these freak fishes (or are they, like whales, mammals?) have cropped up frequently throughout history. Indeed, one cannot help feeling that mankind had some deep-seated desire for there to be something of the sort (just as some sections of the community cling desperately to the idea of flying saucers and Close Encounters). In *Sea Serpents, Sailors and Sceptics*, Mr Graham J. McEwan has listed 600 sightings that have occurred during the past 200 years alone. At least 200 of them can be dismissed as errors or hoaxes, but the remainder, regarded as genuine, cannot be explained.

To begin with, they came in two varieties: the great sea serpent and the mermaid. You do not have to be a sceptic to question the existence of mermaids, which are not to be confused with Sirens. The latter were half woman and half bird, whilst the former were half woman and half fish. The natives of Angola were said to have eaten them, which raised an interesting question. In view of their apparently human content, was this to be regarded as an act of cannabalism? Certainly, in some eastern countries, the inhabitants indulged themselves in a little not altogether innocent deception by attaching the upper parts of monkeys to the tail ends of fishes. All that it required were a length of wire, a certain skill and patience, and an understanding of the gullibility of tourists – to whom they were sold.

If these craftsmen were cynics, the same could not be said of six fishermen from Yell in the Shetland Islands. According to a sworn statement made in 1833, they came across a creature three feet long by about thirty inches in circumference at the broadest point (across the shoulders). From the navel upwards, the body was that of a woman. The only differences were that the fingers were about half the length of a human's and were webbed for about half their length. It had no nose and no ears; its mouth, with white lips that were thicker than average, was large enough to admit a man's fist. Its tail was not unlike that of a halibut. Since it was considered unlucky to kill a mermaid, the fishermen returned it to the sea.

At the time, there seemed to be little doubt that they had actually encountered a mermaid. There were a number of known creatures that, from time to time, had been mistaken for this improbable species, but none of them inhabited the waters surrounding Shetland. So what could the explanation be? For want of anything better, the writer, Mr Tim Dinsdale, suggested that it might have been the result of collective hallucination. It is not entirely satisfactory: Shetland fishermen are not in the habit of hallucinating – individually or collectively. Nor are they in the habit of making false statements, upon oath and before a magistrate. The question remains unsolved.

On the whole, however, it seems that most reports of such encounters can be explained by animals known to exist, or to have existed. Stella's Sea cow, a portly and now probably extinct approximation to a seal, was one favourite. The most likely candidate, however, is the dugong. This amiable mammal has a head that bears a very, very rough resemblance to that of a human being. While suckling one of her young, the female holds it to her breast with a flipper – in much the manner of a human mother. If a dugong is disturbed, she immediately dives underwater, flourishing her fishlike tail. Neither species, however, is likely to have visited the area of the Shetlands. As the land-based creatures of which they are crude caricatures, they prefer warmer waters. In any case, to have mistaken even a dugong for a mermaid suggests that the observers were not very accurate, or else that they were in love with the image of a fish/fair maiden. Certainly, and with the possible exception of the part-monkey-part-fish confidence trick, the concept was put to excellent artistic purpose.

Just as the legend of a flood, an ark, and a chosen survivor was by no means exclusive to the Old Testament, so did several cultures take up the cause of sea serpents. The ultimate example was the theory – or invention, it is hard to say which – of the Scandinavians. Known as Midgaardsormen, it was said to girdle the earth. This seems to have been a rather extravagant claim if the originators hoped to be believed. However, since it was reputed to have led what must have been rather a lonely life on the seabed, the state of the art was not yet ready to disprove the concept.

Later Scandinavians were more moderate in their assertions. An obviously imaginative observer was an eighteenth-century Norwegian missionary in Greenland named Hans Egede. Mr Egede saw his fair share of mermaids (and, come to that, of mermen), but he also reported the existence of the Kraken (or Hafgusa). Wisely, perhaps, he was not too specific in his description – excusing this lapse with the admission that its appearance was 'so terrible and frightful that I do not know how to describe it'. Similarly, he dodged the issue of its dimensions by remarking that they exceeded 'all size and measure'. However, he was in no doubt about its eating habits. It emitted some substance which smelt so pleasantly that fish and even whales gathered round to enjoy it. Having thus assembled the ingredients of its meal, the Kraken swallowed the lot in one big gulp. That, if Egede is to be believed, was good enough to sustain it for a year.

Erik Pontoppidin, Bishop of Bergen, in 1752, embellished the account. The monster, he informed anyone who was interested, had a body about one mile in circumference. But, since it never came completely out of the water, the most that anyone could hope to see of it was its back, which looked rather like a row of small islands. He was vague about its head, contenting himself with the observation that two bright horns extruded from it and that they, in keeping with its gigantic girth, were about the length of masts on a medium-sized ship. He also said that it discharged a mysterious liquid that turned the sea murky (which suggested an outsize octopus). Far from being basically antagonistic to the human race, the Kraken was, in fact, beneficial. Apart from the occasions when one might have mistaken its back for an elongated archipelago, it preferred to live discreetly in the depths – existing on a diet of codfish. This caused any cod that valued its life to come closer to the surface, which made it easier for fishermen to catch them. However, the Bishop counselled caution. The Kraken might become wise to this attempt at evasion and follow the wretched creatures upwards. Under such circumstances, it might very well consume a boatload of fisherfolk by accident – without, indeed, realizing that it had done so.

After that, the Kraken seems to have slept until, very much more recently, that excellent science fiction writer John Wyndham awoke it in his tale *The Kraken Wakes*. Mr Wyndham's views do not appear to have corresponded with those of Bishop Pontoppidin. As anyone who had read this absorbing novel knows, the effect upon mankind was very dire indeed.

Pliny and Aristotle were among the earliest recorders of sea serpents. Whatever they saw cannot have been a sea snake, for the province of these very real creatures is the tropics. They are ten or even twelve feet long and should be avoided. The bite of a cobra is as little more than that of a mosquito compared to their venom. Furthermore, like reptiles on land, their movement is strictly horizontal. Sea serpents, on the other hand, appear to undulate.

Sea serpent observation seems to have been a predominantly northern activity. There was one, or so it was said, that lived beneath the cliffs near Bergen. It was supposed to be 200 feet long, 25 feet in circumference, and had a mane, two feet long, streaming from its head. Its body was covered with scales; its eyes were small and certainly not friendly. Despite its size, it had a strange agility. Without too much trouble it could raise a good deal of itself vertically into the air. This trick had a very practical purpose. It enabled it to remove cattle from islands and, more disturbingly, men from ships. The object, one must assume, was to enrich its supply of food.

In 1746 a gentleman named Kopper sighted something odd six miles off the Norwegian port of Molde. Its head, he asserted, was like that of a horse – with a white mane and black eyes. Its body was a shade of grey. But then Mr Kopper did a foolish thing. Instead of continuing his observations and, possibly, making sketches, he picked up his gun and fired it. The creature obviously knew that it was unwise to hang around when people started discharging firearms, and it slid quietly into the depths. That was the last that he or anyone else saw of it.

The worthy Bishop Pontoppidin endorsed reports of these monstrous worms with enthusiasm. Indeed, such was the reverend gentleman's eagerness for sea serpent sightings, that one feels he was intent upon making them a Norwegian monopoly. There is no telling why – unless he hoped to bring more travellers to his country. After all, whilst hoteliers around the shores of Loch Ness may be inwardly sceptical about the much vaunted monster, it seems unlikely that they would wish it to go away. Where, after all, would Loch Ness *be* without 'Nessie'? Heaven help anyone who can and dares to nail the myth.

But Norway was not to have any such monopoly. At about this time, a Dr Flemming who lived on Orkney saw something off Stronsay which was not entirely dissimilar to the Molde monster. It was, he thought, about 65 feet long, 12 feet in circumference, and capped by a small head mounted on a long neck. No – there were not any scales. But it did have a bristly mane and, so far as he could tell, no fins. Dr Flemming was not the only one to see it. The minister on the island of Eigg in the Hebrides glimpsed something quite similar and so did a number of fishing-boat crews.

Some years later, in 1808, another minister, the Reverend Maclean, was out in his boat off Coll, some miles to the south-west of Eigg. Not far away there was what he at first assumed to be a rock. You can then imagine his amazement when this apparently harmless object suddenly raised itself from the water and regarded him through a pair of yellow eyes. It had, he noticed a thick, sinewy neck and a pair of obviously powerful shoulders. Maclean, profound as his inner search for the truth may have been, did not intend to extend his quest to marine biology – not in this instance at any rate. He bent his back to the oars and rowed off back to the comforting shores of Coll.

Again, there were fishermen nearby to attest the truth of his story. If anything, they had a rather better view. As one of them said afterwards, it was between 70 and 80 feet long, had no fins, and travelled low in the water with an undulating movement. It did not appear to be hostile: indeed, it did not show the least interest in them.

On the far side of the Atlantic, there were also monsters to be seen by anyone who happened to be in the right place at the right time. During the War of Independence, the Reverend Abraham Cummings (it's strange how clergymen keep on cropping up) saw a very weird creature in Penobscot Bay, Maine. According to his calculations, it was 70 feet long and its girth equalled the circumference of an average ship's mast. Some naval officers who also witnessed it put the length at 300 feet, though Mr Cummings accused them of exaggeration. He was also inclined to discount one officer's story that he had seen it leap over a man-of-war.

There is no knowing whether Maclean's monster had relatives on the far side of the Atlantic, or whether it was capable of making its undulating way across the ocean. At all events, there seems to have been a spate of similar sightings on the eastern seaboard of the USA during the early part of the nineteenth century. Whatever was seen did not correspond exactly to the clergyman's account; but, if we make allowances for inaccurate observations, there was a marked similarity.

On a June day in 1815 a man who was taking a stroll along the shore of Gloucester Bay, Massachusetts, saw to his amazement an uncommonly odd creature some yards out to sea. He estimated its length at 100 feet, and remarked that it had something like thirty – or, perhaps, forty – humps. Each was roughly the size of a barrel. Its head was not unlike that of a horse, though larger (six feet, maybe eight, long), and it was dark brown in colour. It was swimming rapidly in a southerly direction.

Two days later it (or one of its kinsmen) reappeared. In this instance, it came within 30 feet of a boat. As it raised its head out of the water, one of the crew fired his gun at it. Either the shot went wide of the mark, or else the visitor's skin was too tough. Whatever the case, it seemed to be uninjured. It turned towards its assailant and appeared to be debating whether or not to attack. Its conclusion must have been that prudence was better than aggression. It dived with remarkable agility and then reappeared about 100 yards away.

During the next year or so, there were several other sightings.

On each occasion, the sea was calm. Sometimes the creature was seen to be taking its ease; sometimes swimming at an estimated twenty miles an hour. Most people agreed that it was 80 or 90 feet long.

In 1818 a gentleman named Tom Prince was looking seawards from a beach near Boston. To his surprise, he saw a creature whose head 'appeared about three feet above the water. I counted thirteen hunches on the back . . . I saw seven distinct views of him, and at some of them the animal was not more than a hundred yards distant.'

A boatload of sailors had a rather less comfortable view. It suddenly reared its head six feet out of the sea and, in a flurry of spray, hurried towards them. But, if its first intention had been to attack, it suddenly reconsidered the matter. It veered away, slowed down and, after making three trips across the bay, headed off towards the open sea.

Not many days later, a Bostonian named Samuel Cabot witnessed something quite similar. 'My intention', Mr Cabot recalled, 'was suddenly arrested by an object emerging from the water at the distance of about one hundred or one hundred and fifty yards, which gave to my mind, at the first glance, the idea of a horse's head. It was elevated about two feet from the water, and he depressed it gradually to within six or eight inches, as he moved along. His humps appeared to me not altogether uniform in size. I felt persuaded by the examination that he could not be less than eighty feet long.'

There were several other glimpses of this strange intruder until 1822, when it – alone or in company of others – seems to have departed. The descriptions varied in matters of detail – the number of humps, for example, ranged from seven to forty, and its length was assessed at anything from 60 to 100 feet. One observer said that it had no eyes; another, that they were 'prominent and stood out boldly from the head'. All the sightings were confined to two bays along the coast: there were no reports from elsewhere.

Despite the fact that most people who witnessed it signed affidavits to this effect, the matter was not taken very seriously. One theory, put forward by J. G. Lockhard in *Mysteries of the Sea* (1924), was that 'The symptoms might be taken to indicate some kind of mass illusion. There is, we believe, a sort of seizure which pathologists term a psychological epidemic, an impulse or an hallucination which attacks bodies of people, frequently recurring at the same season of the year.' Mr Lockhard concluded, 'On the whole, therefore, on this early evidence we should be prudent to regard the existence of the sea serpent as unproved.' To put it another way, he more or less anticipated Mr Dinsdale's verdict on the case of the Shetland fishermen and the mermaid. But, when there is no other hypothesis, what else is there to say?

Sailors might, perhaps, be considered more reliable witnesses, and there is no cause to doubt the story of an uncommonly nasty experience that took place in 1610. A ship was on passage across the Atlantic when the wind dropped and it was becalmed. This, in itself, is strange enough in an ocean noted for its strong winds and high seas. Nevertheless, it is possible. The captain decided to put the delay to good purpose by ordering three men to paint the sides of the hull. They were sitting on a plank suspended on a couple of ropes, quietly going about their business, when the patch of sea beneath them suddenly became turbulent. From the seething water an enormous creature – a giant octopus was how somebody described it – appeared. It stretched out a huge arm, grabbed two of the seamen and then returned in an attempt to snatch the third.

His cries for help were heard by men on the deck above, who attacked the deadly arm with axes and cut it off. The monster did not appear to be in the least discomforted. It continued its assault with single-minded severity. Now the sailors had a go with harpoons. They managed to lift their now terrified companion up on to the deck, which was just as well. The brute was still in full possession of its energies. However, possibly thinking that two members of the mercantile marine were prey enough for one day, it departed. The survivor later became delirious and died that night. Since the hacked-off arm was 25 feet long, as thick as a tree trunk, and covered with suckers the size of saucepan lids, it was hardly surprising. A man can endure just so much shock and no more.

In 1848 the warship HMS *Daedalus* was sailing off the coast of West Africa. The date was 9 July: the sky overcast and the sea undulating in a long swell. The commanding officer, Captain

McQuhae, was on deck when the look-out reported a strange object. As it drew closer, it appeared to be some sort of animal. Its head and shoulders were about four feet above water: it was dark brown in colour with a patch of yellowish-white about the throat. It seemed to have no fins, but a mane, similar to that of a horse, decorated its head.

The creature was travelling quickly, but it passed so close to the ship that it was easy to make out most of the details. McQuhae considered it important enough to report the matter to the Admiralty. In its issue dated 28 October, the *Illustrated London News* gave an account of the episode – enriched by drawings made from McQuhae's description.

At about this time, and a good many miles away, the American ship *Mary Ann* was hove-to, transferring sacks of mail to the brig *Daphne* for delivery at Boston. The master of the *Daphne* recalled that he and his crew had seen a sea monster off the African coast – not far from that observed by the *Daedalus*. In most respects, it tallied with McQuhae's creature, though he supplied the additional information that it appeared to be about 100 feet long. Using a gun loaded with spike-nails and scrap iron, he had fired a shot at it. The sea serpent, as such it was, seemed to be injured. It reared into the air, and then plunged back into the sea. The crew of the *Daphne* lowered a boat in the hope of making a closer investigation. But the object of all this commotion was in no mood for more trouble. It swam off at an estimated speed of 16 knots.

This was all very convincing. However, doubts were cast upon both stories in December of that year. In this case, the *Peking*, commanded by Captain Smith, was about 40 miles from the place in which McQuhae saw his monster. Some distance away there seemed to be an enormously long maritime oddity. 'With our telescopes,' Captain Smith said, 'we could perfectly distinguish an enormous head, and a neck of monstrous size covered with a mane, which apparently appeared and disappeared. This appearance was likewise seen by all our crew, and everybody agreed that it must be the great serpent.'

A boat containing an officer and four men was lowered. They were armed and equipped with a considerable length of rope. 'The monster did not seem disturbed by their approach,' Captain Smith recalled. 'At length they arrived quite close to its head. They appeared to hesitate; then I saw them busily unrolling the rope with which they were provided, while the monster still continued to raise its head and unfold its enormous length.'

It was clearly a very placid creature, for it allowed the men to attach the rope to its neck, and then submitted itself to the ordeal of being towed to the *Peking*. When it was hauled on board, the truth became clear. This was no mysterious inhabitant of the deep, but a very considerable mass of seaweed. And so, too, it was more or less generally agreed, were the phenomena observed from the *Daedalus* and the *Daphne*.

But this did nothing to nail the sea monster myth. On 2 June 1877 the royal yacht *Osborne* (owned by Edward VII when Prince of Wales) was steaming off the north coast of Sicily. At five o'clock in the afternoon, the commanding officer (Captain Pearson) 'distinctly saw a seal-shaped head of immense size, large flippers and part of a huge body'. A Lieutenant Hays, who was also on the bridge, noticed 'a head, two flippers, and about thirty feet of an animal's shoulders'. The head, he estimated, was about six feet thick; the neck narrower – perhaps four or five feet. The creature's shoulders seemed to be about fifteen feet across, and each flipper about fifteen feet long.

Another officer, Lieutenant Forsyth, thought the head was even larger – fifteen or possibly twenty feet long. Whatever its dimensions, this immense seal (if such it was) showed a healthy mistrust of the *Osborne*. It swam off at speed in a south-easterly direction. By the time the Prince had come up to view the stranger, it had vanished.

The end of the nineteenth century was by no means the end of monster sightings. On 7 December 1905 the steamship *Valhalla* was off the coast of Brazil. By a happy coincidence, two Fellows of the Zoological Society were on board. According to one of them, M. J. Nicoll, 'I saw a most extraordinary creature about one hundred yards from the ship moving in the same direction but very much slower than we were going.' The first thing seen by Mr Nicoll and his companion, Mr E. G. B. Meade-Waldo, was a dorsal fin. It was about four feet wide and protruded about two feet from the water. It was brownish-black in colour and could easily have been mistaken for a gigantic piece of ribbon seaweed. However, below the water, it was possible to discern a large patch of something – again brownish-black.

'Every now and then', Mr Nicoll wrote, 'the fin entirely disappeared below water. Suddenly an eel-like neck, about six feet long and of the thickness of a man's thigh, having a head shaped like that of a turtle, appeared in front of the fin. This head and neck, which were the same colour above as the fin, but of silvery-white below, lashed up the water with a curious wriggling movement.' Mr Meade-Waldo's conclusion was that it must have been a giant eel.

Without a doubt, quite a number of supposed sea monster sightings have been the inventions of hoaxers, the products of rather too lively imaginations, or else the misinterpretation of comparatively ordinary phenomena. However, the observations of such experts as Messrs Nicoll and Meade-Waldo deserve to be taken seriously. Nor, one hopes, would the officers of a royal yacht be guilty of an exaggeration intended to deceive.

Arthur Rostron was a mariner of impeccable credentials. As captain of the *Carpathia*, he was responsible for rescuing the survivors of the *Titanic*. Later, he became Cunard's commodore and was rewarded with a knighthood for his services to shipping. Rostron was by no means without imagination, but, ever self-disciplined, he kept it under control. What, then, are we to make of his experience on 26 April 1907?

He was then chief officer of the *Campania*. The liner was off the Irish coast in the vicinity of Cork, when he noticed a strange object sticking out of the water about 50 yards from the ship. He judged its height to be nine feet.

Rostron remembered calling out, 'It's alive.' He wished very badly that he had a camera handy. However, he 'did the next best thing and on the white "dodger board" in front of me I made sketches of the animal, full face and profile, for the thing was turning its head from side to side for all the world as a bird will on a lawn between its pecks.'

Twenty-four years later, a Filey (Yorkshire) coastguard named Wilkinson Herbert saw something not entirely dissimilar. On a moonless night he was walking along a spur of rocks jutting out to sea. 'Suddenly', he told a *Daily Telegraph* reporter, 'I heard a growling like a dozen dogs ahead. Walking nearer, I switched on my torch and was confronted by a huge neck, six yards ahead of me, rearing up eight feet high. The head was a startling sight – huge tortoise eyes, like saucers, glaring at me, the creature's mouth was a foot wide and its neck would be a yard round.

'The monster appeared as startled as I was. Shining my torch along the ground, I saw a body about thirty feet long. I thought, "This is no place for me," and, from a distance, I threw stones at the creature. It moved away growling fiercely, and I saw the huge black body that had two humps on it and four short legs with huge flippers on them. I could not see any tail. It moved quickly, rolling from side to side, and went into the sea. From the cliff top I looked down and saw two eyes like torchlights shining out to sea three hundred yards away.'

A long neck seems to be the common factor of the Rostron and the Herbert sightings. Allowing for exaggeration, either by the original observer or else by the passage of time, does this do anything to make the Bergen sea serpent more credible? Eight or nine feet would confine its cattle rustling activities to low-lying islands, though it would be sufficient to snatch a man from a smallish boat (but why, in this case, did it not appropriate Mr Herbert for a pleasant evening meal? To be deterred by a handful of stones suggests an unadventurous attitude to gastronomic matters). It is, of course, impossible to tell – though it causes one to wonder.

Between the Rostron and the Herbert experiences there was, of course, World War I. One of its casualties seems to have been a creature of many humps that was demolished by gunfire off the coast of Iceland in 1917. The killer was the armed merchant cruiser HMS *Hilary*, an unfortunate ship that, two days afterwards, was sunk by a U-boat. All told, there were seven sea serpent or monster sightings during the years of conflict. One of the more spectacular occurred on 29 July 1915. The *U-38* had just thrust a torpedo into the side of the British steamer *Iberian*, on passage across the North Atlantic with a substantial cargo. The wound was fatal: the merchantman sank and, seconds later, there was a violent explosion as its boilers erupted.

According to the U-boat commander, Freiherr von Forstner, 'A little later pieces of wreckage, and among them a gigantic sea animal, writhing and struggling wildly, were shot out of the water to a height of sixty to one hundred feet.'

The astonished creature seemed to be about sixty feet long, and 'was like a crocodile in shape and had four limbs with powerful webbed feet and a long tail tapering to a point.' However, despite the fact that it was 'gasping and terrified', it seems to have survived and been able to return to its sanctuary many feet beneath the surface. Since, so far as one knows, crocodiles are not inclined to leave their normal stamping grounds for the unkindly waters of the mid-Atlantic, it is hard to know what to make of the story. But von Forstner was by no means the only U-boat commander to witness something of the kind. In July 1918 Werner Lowisch of the *U–109* was tolerably sure that he saw some not dissimilar freak of nature in the North Sea. It had, he alleged, 'a long head, jaws like a crocodile's, and legs with very definite feet.'

Many theories have been advanced to explain these strange creatures often glimpsed by thoroughly reputable eyes. The oar fish (or ribbon fish) has been suggested. It can grow to a length of thirty feet and is more than adequately villainous in appearance. Furthermore, a long dorsal fin, coral red in colour, forms a crest on top of its head – which would explain the 'bristly mane' noticed by Dr Flemming off Stronsay. On the other hand, it is more commonly found in the Mediterranean and prefers to keep to the seclusion of deep waters. Similarly, the giant squid (the Kraken? one wonders) likes to keep itself very far down in the depths, though it has been known to surface, and even to be washed ashore in storms.

Enormous eggs, belonging to some species of eel, have been discovered in the Pacific, and what is an eel if not a serpent? Certainly if one looks at the whale-shark, there is no need to invent a monster. That, fifty feet long and weighing several tons, surely merits such a description. Inevitably, of course, a school of porpoises swimming in line astern has been mistaken for something it certainly was not; and two basking sharks (they tend to travel in pairs) have likewise been misinterpreted by careless observers.

However, in J. R. Norman's *A History of Fishes* (second edition by P. H. Greenwood, D. Sc.), we read: 'Dr Oudemans has published a most valuable book on the subject *The Great Sea-Serpent* (1892), in which nearly all the records are discussed at some length, and the available evidence carefully sifted. He concludes that, although many of the accounts can be disposed of . . . there remains a number which display a certain amount of general agreement and appear to describe something for which none of these theories will really suffice. What this "something" may be can only be guessed, but Dr Oudemans believes it to be a large mammal allied to the Seals and Sea Lions.'

Nearly a century has passed since Dr Oudemans came to this conclusion and the ocean has been greatly explored in this period. Nevertheless, in such an enormity of space, it is foolish to imagine that all its inhabitants have been discovered – or ever will be. To go back to Earth in those early days, reverting to the years when life was evolving (and the chances of *any* life evolving can be assessed at something like one in ten to the power of six hundred against), there were some experiments that succeeded and some that did not. It is, perhaps, nice to think that a few of the less successful essays survive in remote and deep places from which they emerge only very occasionally. Indeed, the very private lives they lead could be the reason why they have survived.

2

Gone Missing

The classic case of a ship vanishing without trace is that of the *Waratah*, a 9,339-ton passenger/cargo vessel owned by the Blue Anchor line. The *Waratah* was employed on the London –Australia route, calling at Cape Town and Durban on the way. On 27 July, 1909 (or it may have been the 28th) she was returning to Britain from Adelaide when, somewhere between the two South African ports, she disappeared. Nothing – no survivors, no debris, not even the smallest clue – was ever discovered. Consequently, to this day, the mystery remains unsolved.

It may seem that the case of the *Waratah* has already been adequately covered. No book of sea mysteries has omitted at least some mention of it. It is, indeed, almost a cliché – as hackneyed as the *Mary Celeste*. Can, then, anything be usefully added to the accounts that have already been published? Is there anything more to be said of the matter? Well: yes, perhaps there is. For, within the greater mystery, there is another. It is a good deal less spectacular and yet it is of considerable significance. Had, at this point, events taken a different turn, the tragedy of the *Waratah* might never have happened.

The ship was built for the Blue Anchor line by Barclay Curle and Company on the Clyde. She was large in terms of such vessels: powered by twin screws and fitted with ·up-to-date equipment. The idea was that, on her voyages to Australia, she would carry emigrants in her holds. On the return trips, they would be replaced by cargo. There was also more comfortable accommodation for first class passengers and the crew. The master, Captain J. E. Ilbery, was commodore of the Blue Anchor Line fleet – a thoroughly experienced mariner who, it might seem, was unlikely to make mistakes. But Captain Ilbery made at least one error – possibly two. He did not, it might seem, listen sufficiently carefully to other people – or, if he did, he did not pass on their opinions to the owners.

When the *Waratah* set off on her maiden voyage in November of the previous year, one of the passengers was Professor William Bragg who occupied the Chair of Physics at Leeds University. The behaviour of the liner in rough seas caused Professor Bragg to be 'very alarmed'. His impression was that the ship's metacentre was in the wrong place. Since its precise situation is essential to a vessel's stability, this was a very serious matter. Although there is no record to this effect, it seems certain that he must have mentioned it to Captain Ilbery. Nor was the chief engineer happy about the *Waratah*'s performance. He judged her to be 'top heavy' and informed his father that he would not be sailing in her on her next voyage. Unhappily, he changed his mind – a decision that cost him his life.

Even in port, the *Waratah* was regarded as a 'tender' ship – which means to say that, when unloaded, she couldn't be manoeuvred without ballast. Furthermore, there is evidence to suggest that, when she rolled, she seemed sluggish in her reaction; and, when at last she recovered herself, she did so with an unpleasant jerk – a movement that was apt to throw unwary passengers rather violently on to the deck.

Inevitably, after that maiden voyage, the owners should have asked Captain Ilbery his opinion of his new charge. Certainly he mentioned a small fire that had broken out in one of the bunkers due to insufficient insulation. The matter was put right at Sydney and it was a thing of no great importance. Apart from this, the management of the Blue Anchor Line do not seem to have questioned him in any great detail. Nor does he appear to have been very forthcoming. He remarked that she was a 'comfortable' ship, and so she may have been in terms of her furnishings. But nicely appointed accommodation is of little value in a probably unstable environment.

Nevertheless, if Captain Ilbery had any doubts, he kept them to himself. The ship was drydocked; a team of Lloyds surveyors examined her hull and pronounced it seaworthy; and she was prepared for her next voyage. It seems improbable that they concerned themselves with such things as metacentres. As for Professor Bragg, his mind was doubtless now preoccupied with other, more academic, matters.

On 27 April 1909 the *Waratah* sailed from London on her second round voyage to Australia. The outward passage passed with neither incident nor comment. After calling at several Australian ports, she sailed from Adelaide on 7 July and arrived at Durban on the 25th. For a report on what happened during this leg of the trip, we are indebted to a businessman named Claude G. Sawyer. Mr Sawyer had bought a ticket to Cape Town and consequently should have been one of the ship's victims. But a number of things happened to cause him to change his mind. Instead, he came ashore at Durban and completed his journey by some other means.

He later insisted that he had overheard the third officer remarking on the *Waratah*'s top-heaviness. While taking a bath in rough weather, he noticed that the ship was rolling over to an angle that he estimated to be 45 degrees. The jerk that was such a feature of the ship's recovery from these excesses was most marked; and, indeed, a number of passengers were injured by falls. To make no bones about it, Mr Sawyer was disturbed by this apparent instability and his misgivings were reinforced by a dream he experienced three times running. There are several different versions of it, but the gist of it was that a man, wearing some kind of unusual garb, was standing at the end of his bunk. In one hand he held a sword, which he pointed at Mr Sawyer; in the other, a rag that had been soaked in blood. To this imaginative man of commerce, there was no mistaking the message. If he valued his life, he should go ashore at the first opportunity and never mind the rest of the trip to Cape Town. He had to forfeit the balance of his fare, but this was a small price for his life.

(At this point, one wonders what was so singular about Claude G. Sawyer that he, of all the 211 souls aboard the *Waratah*, was singled out for survival. But that is how it was.)

The *Waratah* topped up her supplies of coal at Durban, took on 248 tons of cargo (she was now carrying more than 10,000 tons) and, with 92 passengers on board, departed on the 26th. At

6 o'clock on the following morning, she overhauled the freighter *Clan MacIntyre*, exchanged polite signals, and that was the last that was ever seen of her.

If you should ever compile a list of the areas of the world's oceans that pose dreadful hazards to shipping, the route from Durban to Cape Town would appear somewhere near the top. When a local depression moves in an east north-easterly direction, it generates violent westerly winds that produce waves between 20 and 30 feet high and 180 to 270 feet long. Any vessel that ploughs into them head-on is liable to be in serious trouble.

Something of the kind was brewing in this instance. The master of the *Clan MacIntyre* afterwards recalled that, in all his thirteen years in the trade, he had never experienced anything quite so bad on this particular coast. However, he also remarked that, as she overtook him at 13 knots, he did not notice anything remarkable about the *Waratah*. She appeared, he said, 'to be proceeding in an exceedingly steady manner.'

Perhaps she was – at that time. But although several other ships passed that way, and although, after she became overdue at Cape Town, a thorough search was mounted, nothing more was ever seen of the pride of the Blue Anchor Line. There have been many theories about what might have happened to her. The most likely seems to be that she hit one of these enormous waves and that, while still reeling from the impact, another struck her. This was too much and the *Waratah* foundered. However it has to be recorded that, despite winds of hurricane force, no harm befell the *Clan MacIntyre* nor any of the other vessels. One reason might have been that such rogue waves are so very local that they may pass unnoticed by another vessel in the vicinity. One cannot, however, discount all those doubts about the *Waratah*'s stability. Perhaps she just wasn't ship enough to withstand such extreme punishment. This, of course, takes us back to the other mystery. Why did Captain Ilbery not express his doubts when he returned from the maiden voyage? Was he really satisfied with the behaviour of his new command? One has to wonder.

The *Waratah* was, we are assured, equipped with up-to-date navigational aids and machinery. But it has to be remembered that 'up-to-date' had a very different meaning in 1909 to that of nowadays. When starting to plan a book of this nature, it is tempting to make the most of these oldish tales in the wild assumption (which no sailor would make) that such mysteries do not occur in this age of high technology. But they do. The *Waratah* probably went to her doom so suddenly that, even had the means been available, there would have been no time in which to send out a distress signal. Aircraft (surely the highest tech of all in terms of transportation) have sometimes been in this situation – one has only to look at the Air India 747 that crashed into the Atlantic in June 1985 to see this. The truth is that vessels still go missing without trace – and possibly always will do. The fact that the *Waratah* has become some sort of legend must partly be due to the fact that she had passengers aboard, and partly to Mr Sawyer who, having enjoyed the heady experience of survival, turned out to be extremely talkative. Presumably he did dream those dreams: they certainly did nothing to take the edge off his narrative. Nowadays, the victims tend to be less glamorous: cargo vessels, some of them huge and lumbering, that are expunged, nobody quite knows where, from the ocean's surface. Despite the development of electronic gadgetry, the sea must have its sacrificial offerings. And the sea receives them.

Since records were first kept by Lloyds in the mid-1860s, a prodigious 4,083 vessels have been officially posted as missing. Between 1980 and 1985, sixteen ships disappeared without trace. The total tonnage added up to 400,000 and, between them, they accounted for 400 lives. The causes can only be matters of conjecture: freak weather conditions, explosions, shifting cargoes and even piracy have all been mooted as possible culprits. The fact that some passed with only the smallest mention in the press did not diminish their tragedy nor their mystery. After all, if you are related to one of the victims, it matters little whether the total toll is five or five thousand. Indeed, if you study the appropriate issue of *The Times* for a mention of the *Mary Celeste* affair (admittedly a case of missing persons rather than a missing ship), you have to search for the report, which was thought to merit only a column inch or two. It did not become celebrated until about twelve years later, when Arthur Conan Doyle used it as a peg upon which to hang a story entitled 'J. Habakuk Jephson's Statement' – published in the *Cornhill Magazine* (and, incidentally beginning the erroneous habit of calling the hermaphrodite brig *Marie Celeste*).

All too rarely some of these mysteries are eventually solved. On 20 February 1899 the sailing ship *Red Rock* of Glasgow put out from Townsville in Queensland, Australia, on passage for Noumea in New Caledonia – a voyage of about a thousand miles. A crew of 24 was on board. On 27 February she was sighted off Magnetic Island, or such was the assertion. Since this small piece of land is not very far from Townsville, she was either wrongly identified, or else she had made uncommonly slow going. After that, she seemed to disappear. She was posted as 'missing' by Lloyds on 6 June and the appropriate documents for making insurance claims were prepared. They were about to be signed when, six days later and to everybody's amazement, a telegram arrived from the ship's master, Captain Potter. Apparently, he had at last reached Noumea. The weather, it seemed, had been appalling: he had lost a great deal of gear and several of his sails – but, in the end, he made it. This is the only occasion on which a vessel designated as 'missing' by Lloyds has actually turned up. Usually the word means exactly what it says.

The Second World War produced considerable advances in aids to navigation: radar and such systems as Loran and Decca. Indeed, as early as 1945 a scientist was predicting the advent of satellites as a means of communication. In theory, these developments might have marked the end of mysteriously missing ships – or, at any rate, a sharp decline in their number. But the ocean and its ally in villainy, the weather, were not to be defeated. Nor, when one considers it, can this be seen as surprising. Against man's ingenuity, the two can mass a force so strong that it is hard to imagine. What is more, they are devious in their tactics and can confound even the most sophisticated forecasting methods. After all, the invention of wireless a good many years earlier should, at least, have given a captain in trouble the opportunity to transmit a distress signal. But in some cases the attack was so sudden and so severe that there was no time in which to tap out those most simple of all the letters in the Morse alphabet, sos.

Whatever her virtues, the British India Steam Navigation Company's *Sir Harvey Adamson* was an old ship. She registered only 1,030 tons, and, for the better part of thirty-three years, had been going about her business in the Far East. In 1947, she was employed on the run from Rangoon, along the coast of Burma and so to the ports of Tavoy and Mergui near the Malaysian frontier. Some merchantmen had already benefited from the technologies that were the compensation for war, but not the *Sir Harvey Adamson*. Whilst no doubt maintained to the highest possible standards, she was nonetheless much the same as she had been on her maiden voyage in 1914 – the same and yet a great deal older.

On 17 April, 1947 this small veteran, this hack of the high seas, sailed from Rangoon on what should have been just another journey on the milk run. On board her were 17 saloon and 188 deck passengers, plus a crew of nine Europeans, 54 Indians, and one solitary Chinaman. Next day, she was sighted off Bilugyun, an island that lies at the approaches to Moulmein on the eastern side of the Gulf of Martaban. A strongish wind was blowing, but nothing seemed to be amiss. But that, nevertheless, was the last that was seen of the *Sir Harvey Adamson*. A few items of wreckage that could be identified with the ship were later washed up on the coast of Burma. But of the 269 souls that had sailed in her, there was not the slightest trace.

The assumption was that, with the weather worsening, she foundered in a gale. Had it not been for meagre evidence of the debris, the tragedy might have been compared with that of the *Waratah*. The casualty list was longer to the extent of an extra 58 missing persons. The waters in which the *Sir Harvey Adamson* went about her business had no such evil reputation as those in which the *Waratah* shed her mortal coil. In the Blue Anchor liner's favour so far as legend-making was concerned was the fact that she was a young vessel, that she had the decency to vanish without any trace whatsoever, and that the timing was better. She disappeared during a long period of maritime peace (the Boer War, whilst bad enough in all conscience, was not notable for its naval engagements). The British India ship, on the other hand, was lost soon after a conflict in which the public mind had become almost numbed by the number of casualties inflicted by enemy action. For a vessel to go missing, especially such a small one as this, was no longer considered remarkable.

As this may suggest, the dividing line between a sea mystery and a marine disaster without any eerie overtones is a fine one. One essential, however, is that the ocean shall erase all evidence – human or otherwise. For example, the Norwegian ore and oil carrier, *Berge Istra*, does not qualify for inclusion in the former category. Nevertheless, she deserves to be mentioned as an example of what one may, perhaps, describe as a 'near miss'.

The *Berge Istra* was a very big ship indeed. With a deadweight tonnage of 223,963, she was a fair representative of a new breed of vessel that had made its first appearance in the 1960s. In the press, they were described as 'super-tankers' – an epithet that their owners may have lived to regret. Nowadays, you can find many of them laid up in estuaries – either waiting in the scrapyard queue, or else surviving in the forlorn hope that, one day, they may come in useful once more.

A couple of factors caused the birth of the super-tanker. One was the catastrophic business of 1956, when President Nasser of Egypt decided to take over the Suez Canal; Israel went on the rampage against Egypt by invading the Sinai Peninsular; Britain and France joined in by occupying the canal zone; America, pointedly, did nothing; and Nasser blocked the canal to shipping. As a result, supplies of crude oil from the Arabian Gulf had to be routed to Europe by way of the Cape of Good Hope. Under these circumstances, the larger the load a vessel could carry, the better it would be. Furthermore, the shipping fraternity was rediscovering a truth propounded a century earlier by Isambard Kingdom Brunel when he conceived the *Great Eastern*. The gist of it was that, far from being more costly to operate than a smaller ship, a large one was, in fact, more economical.

So there we were in December 1975, with the *Berge Istra* – the product of a Yugoslav shipyard and built in 1972 – on passage 170 miles to the south-west of Mindanao in the Philippines. The sea was relatively calm and none of her 32-man crew had any cause for anxiety. And then, quite suddenly, it happened. Within the space of three minutes or so, a massive, well-ordered ship vanished. Her value was estimated at $27 million and her cargo of iron ore, in transit from Tubarao, Brazil, to Kimitsu in Tokyo Bay, at $9 million. The human content was beyond price.

Once the *Berge Istra*'s existence (or, rather, apparent lack of it) had begun to worry her owners in Oslo, aircraft flew innumerable sorties without discovering the smallest sign of her. If she had foundered, that was undoubtedly that. The sea here is something like six miles deep. Quite apart from the impossibility of conducting salvage operations at this depth, the very pressure would have reduced the carrier to the merest fraction of her former size. The fact that the *Berge Istra* was now qualified for admission to the record books as the largest-ever marine casualty did little to comfort anyone. To lose her was bad enough; for the mystery to be unexplained was to compound the disaster. Although the area in which she had last been reported is notorious for its storms, there was no storm raging at the time. Although there were more than sufficient vessels flying flags of convenience – vessels that were unseaworthy and manned by personnel barely competent to navigate a rowing boat on an urban lake – the *Berge Istra* was well founded and her crew were thoroughly able. Quite simply, the disaster should not have occurred.

But then, nineteen days after she had disappeared, the matter was solved. A Japanese fishing boat, the *Hachiho Maru Number 6*, came across a raft 100 miles from the point at which the *Berge Istra* had disappeared. On board it were two very exhausted Spanish seamen. They were taken to the US Air Force base at Okinawa where, suitably refreshed and comforted, they told their stories.

It transpired that on her previous voyage she had carried a cargo of crude oil to Rotterdam. Her wing tanks had been cleaned and filled with inert gas. However, these precautions do not seem to have been sufficient. If the Spaniards were to be believed, there had been a massive explosion (probably in a wing tank just forward of the bridge), which had caused the ship to list. A second had followed about fifteen seconds later, and a third about thirty seconds after that. The two survivors had been part of a team of five engaged in painting the fore deck. They had been flung into the water and, within a very short time, they saw the fragmented giant slide into the depths.

One of them noticed a liferaft and swam towards it. He was joined by an injured companion to whom he gave first aid. Of the other three – and, indeed, of everyone else on board the *Berge Istra* – there was no trace. There were, however, plenty of items of food floating about and they were able to scoop up a sufficient supply to keep them going. For water, they had to depend on rain.

The mystery was solved – more or less. But one is still left with the question of the explosion. All that should have been done after discharging that cargo of crude at Rotterdam had, or so it seems, been accomplished. She had crossed the ocean to Brazil without anything untoward occurring, loaded a cargo of iron ore, and then sailed an even greater distance to the vicinity of the Philippines. Days, weeks, had gone by without any hint of the enemy that lurked within – until, in a fraction of a second, some kind of ignition had occurred and blown the giant to pieces. What is the explanation for that? For God's sake, why did the *Berge Istra* have to die, and take thirty people with her?

It may seem ironic that a nation with such a distinguished history of seafaring as Norway should have twice topped the record charts for the largest ship to go missing. (The *Titanic*, for example, was not eligible to compete in this unpleasant contest. There may be a lesser puzzle about her captain's state of mind – about why, despite warnings, he failed to take suitable precautions, and about why he was feasting with the passengers when, all too obviously, he should have been on the bridge. But there is no mystery about the ship herself: the wheres and whys of the disaster are perfectly comprehended.) The *Berge Istra*, mystery though she may not completely be, inherited her dark distinction from a Cypriot ore carrier named the *Theodore AS* that vanished in the North Sea with a cargo of iron ore which was loaded at Narvik and should have arrived at Gijon in Spain. Since there were severe gales storming in from the west at the time, it is almost certain that she was overwhelmed by high seas. But no wreckage was ever found and the case must be marked UNPROVEN. That was in 1973. On 21 March of that year, the 12,946-ton Norwegian freighter *Anita* sailed from Hampton Roads, Virginia, with a cargo of coal. Her destination should have been Bremen. But storm force winds were lashing the North Atlantic into a fury that was remarkable even for such a furious place as this. Like the *Theodore AS*, she was almost beyond reasonable doubt destroyed by the sea; but, for want of evidence, no prosecutor would have been able to secure a conviction. The *Norse Varient* was also outward bound from Hampton Roads but, in this instance, travelling towards Glasgow with coal. She disappeared on the day following the *Anita*'s departure. In this case, however, the hypothetical jury need have been in no doubt about the perpetrator. Against all the laws of probability, a survivor was eventually picked up. He described how, storm battered and virtually out of control, the vessel had broken in two and sank 130 miles south-east of Cape May, New Jersey. Thus, the *Anita*'s record remained. In any case, the two ships were much of a size. They both disappeared on the same day (the 22nd) and each accounted for thirty lives.

One of the more singular cases of a missing ship, and one that gave rise to wild speculation, was that of the *Milton Iatridis*. Originally named the *Glimmingehus*, the tanker had been built in 1952 for a Swedish company named Trelleborg. Later she was sold to the World Wide Group of Hong Kong, which changed her name to *World International*. In 1968 she came on to the market again and was bought by a Greek firm. It was on this occasion that she became the *Milton Iatridis*.

At the beginning of November 1969 the *Milton Iatridis* sailed from Canvey Island in the Thames estuary with a cargo of caustic soda. She docked at New Orelans, where a consignment of soya bean oil was added to the manifest. On the 14th she departed across the South Atlantic for Kwinana in Western Australia. From there, she should have proceeded to Chittagong in Pakistan. But she never reached either port. Somewhere in the vastness of the ocean, she disappeared.

Her last reported position was received on 28 November. She was, apparently, just south of the equator and just less than half way across. However, this may not have been her final resting place. Later reports were received of a ship that might have been the *Milton Iatridis*. On this evidence, she was still alive and well after travelling many miles farther south and well to the west – not all that far, really, from the coast of South Africa.

Whatever the truth of the matter, the hapless tanker and all who sailed in her vanished from the face of the ocean. For want of any better explanation, there were a number of assumptions that she had either been hijacked, or else that, of her crew's own accord, she had defected to Cuba. The first was simply wild speculation without a shred of reason behind it. The second was easily discounted. Had she been going to Cuba, her master had taken an almighty out-of-the-way route. In any case, there were no accounts of a vessel answering to her description turning up in, say, Havana – and no reasonable explanation for any such action.

A much more probable hypothesis is that she was unsuited to the transport of caustic soda, and that the chemical had eaten its way through her steel plates. The *coup de grace* may have been administered by an explosion.

Between January 1961 and December 1971, no fewer than 70 vessels were officially reported as 'missing' by Lloyds of London. In none of these cases was the cause determined beyond *any* reasonable doubt – though, in several, there were some pretty shrewd surmises. The rest of the 1970s added to the score, and the first half of the 'eighties did little to suggest that the ocean had become a place into which a mariner could venture without any misgivings. In an issue of *Chart and Compass International* (published by the British Sailors' Society), the editor reported that 'Sixteen vessels with a total tonnage of 400,000 tons, and approaching 400 crew members, have vanished without trace in the vast oceans of the world in the past five years.'

'The sea', he wrote, 'is still a place of grim secrets and baffling mysteries and those who sail upon it and experience its many moods must still be men of courage and faith.' There used to be a prayer uttered by ancient Phoenician fishermen which contained the words, 'Oh Lord, Thy sea is so great and my ship is so small'. In comparison with the oceans upon which it sails, *any* ship is small and even the greatest strength becomes puny when pitted against the huge forces of wind and water. The trouble, perhaps, is that, in their snug offices upon land, there are still too many people who prefer to ignore this very simple truth. Commerce rules: the businessman's chart is a balance sheet. If a vessel can be constructed more cheaply by cutting a few corners, it will take less time to write off the initial investment and the god of profit will be satisfied. Such an attitude may not apply to all nations or to all owners, but it exists just the same. Nor is there anything new about it. History is littered with wrecks that, if not deliberately contrived, were nonetheless quietly applauded. Unseaworthy vessels, badly equipped, were dispatched into waters for which they were totally inadequate. If they failed to return, and if times were hard, the insurance money provided more than adequate compensation for the surrender to the sea of a loss-making hulk. Admittedly, this form of callous fraud is no longer indulged in by western nations, but some owners in Third World countries are not above having a go.

In this respect, the shipping industry and those who govern it internationally come off badly in comparison with the aviation industry. In the case of a crashed aircraft, the investigation is prompt, there are seldom attempts to conceal its findings, and anything that is discovered and may, perhaps, prevent such a disaster from recurring, is quickly made known. Every commercial aeroplane is equipped with a so-called 'black box' (it isn't black, really, and, in any case there are two of them – but never mind) which can supply the investigators with vital clues about what occurred during the minutes and seconds before an accident. In theory, ships can be equipped with something very similar. It would float away from the wreck and a radio beacon would enable it to be discovered by a search and rescue aircraft. In practice, very few vessels indeed are provided with this apparatus.

According to an official of the National Union of Seamen, air safety has increased by at least five per cent during the past few years; safety at sea by one per cent. This is particularly disturbing when one considers that the high technology which has assisted the former cause has also been available to the latter. The difference is – and setting aside the matter of cruise liners – that aeroplanes rely mostly upon human lives for their freight. Ships do not. The fact that some cargoes are capable of further contaminating an already contaminated environment is apt to be ignored. So, too, is the fact that they are manned by crews, and what are they if not human lives?

There was a time, in the days of the great passenger liners, when big was considered to be beautiful – and (despite the *Titanic* experience) safe. When a new giant such as the *Queen Mary* was produced, illustrated magazines used to print drawings of how she might look if placed in the centre of London – usually in the vicinity of Trafalgar Square, with Nelson's Column reaching up to about the level of the boat deck. Since those more glamorous days, very much larger vessels have been built, but they are different. Basically, they are like stupendously large lighters, fitted with engines and with an accommodation block perched on top somewhere near the stern. The hulls are constructed under cover in sections – which are transported to the slipway and welded together. You couldn't quite do the same thing with a mammoth Lego set; but, in appearance at any rate, you might get somewhere near it.

Any ideas that size equals complete safety were demolished by the loss of the *Berge Istra*; by that of the 216,326 deadweight tons Liberian tanker *Golar Pacific*, which sank on 5 November 1973, 130 miles off the Canary islands (and thereby achieved a kind of immortality by appearing in the *Guinness Book of Records*); and, more recently,, by the disappearance of the Bibby Tankers' MV *Derbyshire* (169,044 tons deadweight: more about her in a later chapter).

Within the cluster of the early 'eighties casualties, there were, admittedly, quite a number of small vessels. On 5 January 1981, for example, the 1,569 tons gross West German motorship *Rugwardersand* sailed from Leghorn (Livorno) with a cargo of flour for Annaba in Algeria. She never arrived. The only traces ever discovered were some flour bags floating in the strait between Corsica and Sardinia. The ship was only two years old. The crew of ten (possibly fifteen: the records are uncertain) vanished with her. On 6 May of that year the 1,205 tons gross *Wheststar* departed from Santander in Spain with her holds filled with cement. She, too, was West German. Fourteen days later, she vanished somewhere to the north of the Azores. On 17 June 1981 the little Greek motorship *Delta* of 957 tons gross left Gabes, Tunisia, bound for Alexandria with a cargo of aluminium fluoride. In the seven years of her lifetime, the *Delta* had been the property of four owners – and had been known by four names: the *Sea King 1*, the *Lone Lion*, the *Greif*, and, of course, the *Delta*. It was as the *Delta* that she died. Having cleared the mouth of Gabes harbour, she was neither seen nor heard from again. And so on: it should be remembered that we are dealing only with ships that have vanished – this is not a tally of wrecks.

Some gave notice of their going, which usually served to explain – unofficially, at any rate – their disappearances. For instance, the 25,200 tonnes deadweight *Dunav*, flying the Yugoslavian flag, left Hamilton, Ontario, on 20 October 1980. She was carrying steel products, newsprint and general goods intended for Tsingtao in China. When she was 700 miles to the south-east of Chiba in Japan, her master reported that she was battling against very rough seas and taking in an alarming amount of water. He proposed, he said, to divert from his course and make for Yokahama. That was the last anyone heard of the *Dunav* or her crew of thirty-two.

A similar case was that of the Panamanian *Arctic Carrier*, a bulk carrier of 69,389 tonnes deadweight, that had left Tubarao, Brazil, on 17 June 1984. Later that month, she radioed her agents, Prompt Shipping of Hong Kong: 'Encountered boisterous weather with wind north-west Force 9, June 23. Following damage found . . .' There followed a sorry list of distorted bulkheads, at least one faulty hatch coaming, and blemishes in the adjacent deck plating. That was the last anyone heard from her. A few items of wreckage, a small oil slick, and several drums were seen by searching aircraft three hundred miles to the north-east of that lonely Atlantic island, Tristan da Cunha. Of the *Arctic Carrier* there was no trace. According to *Lloyd's List*, 'The most popular theory behind her apparent loss is that shift of cargo had caused her to "corkscrew" and break-up in the fierce seas running in the region at this time of the year. Again, the almost total lack of evidence means that the real reason for her loss, which must have been as unexpected as sudden, will probably remain a mystery.' One supposes so – though the contents of that radio signal suggest that it was neither 'unexpected' nor 'sudden'. If it was, the master must have been a remarkable optimist.

The *Orient Treasury*, which had begun her life as the *Geralton Maru* when she was built in 1966, was a stranger case. This 28,776-ton bulk carrier flying the Panamanian flag, was carrying chrome ore insured for $2.9 million when she sailed from Masinlok in the Philippines on 12 January 1982. She was on course for Uddevalla in Sweden with a crew of twenty-six on board. On 9 February she reported that she had called at Port Said and those were her last words. The Panamanian authorities went through the motions of an investigation and concluded, for want of any other evidence, that she might have been a victim of piracy. Well: why not? Whatever anyone may tell you, there is still a lot of it about – though the targets are mostly yachts and other pleasure craft. On the face of it, chrome ore may not appear to be very exciting plunder. However, when one looks into the matter more deeply, one finds that it has a military application (something to do with steel). If this was the case, it does not suggest the villainy of some opportunist buccaneer, but of an unfriendly power (unfriendly to whom?) that had the means to use the substance. Whatever the merits of the idea, however, it leaves several loose ends. What, for example, became of the ship? Was she scuttled – 28,776-tons' worth of bulk carrier is not easy to hide? And what was the fate of her crew? Were they killed, or were they accomplices? For those who prefer stories with tidy endings, the case of the *Orient Treasury* is far from satisfactory.

For an owner to lose one ship is a misfortune. To lose two within a comparatively short space of time is apt to arouse suspicion. In June 1985 two vessels belonging to the Maini Shipping Company of India went missing in the Bay of Bengal. On 18 June the freighter *Nitya Nanak* (5,850 tonnes gross) was on passage from Colombo in Sri Lanka with a cargo of salt for Calcutta. On 21 June she reported her position for the last time. After that, no further word was heard from her – nor from her crew of twenty-two.

Meanwhile, the *Nitya Ram* (5,692 tonnes and also manned by a crew of twenty-two) had sailed from Calcutta loaded with coal for Tuticorin in Madras. She, too, disappeared. Despite a search that continued until early July, no traces of either vessel were ever discovered. An investigation was ordered by the Indian authorities: the remainder of the Maini Shipping Company's fleet – three ships and three inland barges – were brought into port for a check-up on their seaworthiness.

But, when the matter was examined in greater detail, a number of oddities were revealed. The *Nitya Nanak*, it seemed, had put into Colombo for repairs to her communications equipment and her radar. She departed on the night of the

18th/19th. On the 20th, her master, Captain K. R. Puri radioed the owners: 'Fresh holes developed in Number One hold. Water rushing in.' At 6pm on the following day, he reported that the situation had worsened and that he proposed to make for Madras. The shipping company's management, it seems, questioned the necessity for this and told him to keep on course for Calcutta. However, a representative stressed that the actual words had been: 'Relying on you to proceed to Calcutta direct.' This, he insisted had not been an order – it was up to Captain Puri to take whatever action seemed suitable. In any case, the message was never received. It was not until five days later that the Mercantile Marine Department was informed that the *Nitya Nanak* had vanished.

The *Nitya Ram*, commanded by Captain Sharma, sailed from Calcutta on 17 June with 5,182 tons of coal on board. At 10am on the 18th, Captain Sharma reported that his vessel was taking in water in one of the holds. However, at 9.20am on the following day, the trouble appeared to have been overcome. The master could, he said, cope with the situation. All too obviously he could not. The ship was due at Tuticorin on 25 June. It was not until the 27th, however, that the agent in Madras showed any signs of anxiety and not until the 28th that he notified the Principal Officer of the Mercantile Marine Department. Coast Guard and naval ships explored the *Nitya Ram*'s route and found nothing. Nor did a search by aircraft covering a radius of two hundred miles.

Reporting the losses, The Missions to Seamen's newspaper *The Sea* commented that 'The coincidences of the disappearances, the lack of an obvious cause, the failure to send distress calls, and the absence of any trace of ships or crew, have led to speculations of fraud and hijacking. The possibility of fraud is being investigated by the International Maritime Bureau in London. Relatives of the missing seafarers feel they are still alive, and hopes have been encouraged by mysterious telephone calls saying that the *Nitya Nanak* had been hijacked.' There is still no evidence to support this view, and one has to consider that the telephone calls may have been cruel hoaxes.

A search for common factors between these disappearances does not produce anything likely to be helpful. Two of the ships were less than five years old: the majority were between seven and twenty-one years old. Ten of them were carrying cargoes of ore or other metal products that were liable to become unstable in severe weather. The others were loaded with a miscellaneous selection of commodities – flour, grain, cement, and so on. One of them was travelling in ballast. Six of them went missing in an area of the Pacific around Japan and the Philippines; but, of them, only two vanished during the height of the July–October typhoon season. Two losses in the Caribbean did, admittedly, occur during the August–October peak hurricane period for that corner of the ocean. On the other hand, three were lost in the Atlantic off Spain and Portugal. The worst storms here occur between November and March. The unfortunate trio did not disappear during these furious months. Since 1980, none of the vanished vessels had been carrying anything likely to explode, or to release toxic fumes when it came into contact with sea water. And, apart from the case of the *Orient Treasury* any ideas of piracy can be set aside.

Of all the possible causes, freak weather conditions seem to be the most likely. The incorrect loading of bulk carriers also suggests itself. In some cases, the crew may have been at fault; in others, the actual design of the ship.

The Blue Anchor liner *Waratah* secured herself a place in history. The other vessels mentioned in this chapter – with the exception of the *Derbyshire* – have been forgotten by the majority of people. And yet they, in many ways, are the more surprising. There have been such massive advances in technology since the day when those 211 people died in the unquiet seas off the south-east coast of Africa. The trouble appears to be that a not inconsiderable part of the shipping industry seems to be too parsimonious to invest in them.

3

The Fire Bug

Whether or not the *Morro Castle* was a happy ship depended upon who you were. The chances were that, if you were a passenger, you found the food excellent, the appointments luxurious, and the service reasonable. If, on the other hand, you were a member of the crew, you were probably less than contented. The pay was poor, the conditions a lot less than satisfactory, and the diet, even to an insensitive palate, excruciating. However, there were certain compensations. The Ward Line, which owned this 11,520-ton vessel, was undoubtedly an unsatisfactory employer. This might, perhaps, be explained (some might say 'excused') by a simple economic truth: the lower the overheads, the greater the profit. On the other hand, the *Morro Castle* ran a service between New York and Cuba. For anyone engaged in such trade during the 1930s, there were ample opportunities to conduct illicit transactions as a sideline. Whatever President Castro's faults may be, he appears, so to speak, to have tidied up the island. When the *Morro Castle* went about her business in great waters, Havana was a place of intrigue; a market place for narcotics in transit from the rest of the world to the United States; and a point of departure from which anyone unsure of a rapturous welcome by the US emigration authorities might gain access to the promised land.

The *Morro Castle*'s complement (or most of them) were engaged in all these small services to the darker side of mankind. When stubbornly refusing to recognize trade unions, the Ward Line's management might have wondered why it should provide fair wages and diet for the job, since many of those engaged in it were, by their own enterprise, making good such deficiencies. With no disrespect to that noble calling, it was as if an hotel might question the need to pay its hall porter, say, £5,000 a year, when he is receiving £15,000 *p.a.* in tips.

For those who like to know about such things, the *Morro Castle* was built in 1930 by the Newport News Shipbuilding and Drydock Company in Virginia. Her turbo-electric engines gave her a service speed of 20 knots: her comparatively luxurious accommodation provided quarters for 430 first class passengers and 100 who elected, whether by choice or from straitened circumstances, to travel tourist.

On 1 September 1934, the *Morro Castle* departed from her berth at New York for a so-called 'Labor Day Cruise' to Havana. Her master was Captain Robert Wilmott, a Ward Line veteran of thirty-one years standing. In the company of passengers he was genial, out-going, all the things that the model master mariner of a passenger ship should be. To the crew, he was a mite less affable, though this is not hard to understand. By all accounts, this chubby and capable man of the sea wanted to run what they call a tight ship. Unfortunately the only things about this unhappy vessel that deserved the adjective (albeit in a different sense) were many of the passengers and likewise the personnel. But, when rum could be bought in Cuba for the very reasonable sum of four dollars a gallon, it was, one dares say, understandable. After all, the land of the free had only recently been released from a sentence of thirteen years prohibition. Such an ordeal is apt to leave its mark upon a thirsty citizen.

Whilst Captain Wilmott seems to have tolerated the import of firearms to Cuban rebels (somewhat euphemistically labelled 'sporting goods'), he was less than ready to countenance the smuggling of drugs. From time to time, he ventured into the quarters of his crew with the zeal of a narcotics officer. But such excursions did little to decrease the trade – nor did they improve his popularity. He might, indeed, have been better employed in another area: an area that should have claimed a shipmaster's attention and in which the lame excuse that it might frighten the passengers is not worth serious consideration. It was, ironically as things turned out, fire fighting.

If weather conditions pose the ultimate hazard from without, fire is the potential enemy from within. The Chief Officer of the *Morro Castle*, William F. Warms, had an above-average awareness of this: an awareness, you might say, that had been forced upon him. Some years previously, he had been in command of a freighter owned by the Ward Line. Ignoring the company's regulations, he had neglected to carry out fire drills. Word of this oversight got around and Warms was brought to book. In retribution for his lapse, he was suspended for eighteen months. The punishment had obviously been salutary, for nobody on board the liner had a greater respect for such procedures than this once errant officer. Unhappily, in this respect, he received no encouragement from his captain. Wilmott, presumably considering himself immune from such disciplinary action, did not hold fire drills – and nor did he make sure that the equipment to combat a blaze was properly checked. One might have imagined that the customers would have found the crew's attention to such essential details reassuring. Wilmott disagreed. It could, he decided engender panic. Not to put too fine a point upon it, he appears to have been obsessive in his determination not to provoke any kind of fear.

Wilmott didn't care much for Warms, which may be understandable. The latter does not seem to have worn the air of authority that becomes a chief officer. Indeed, he appears to have had the kind of mind that, when confronted by a confusion of difficulties, finds itself unable to focus on any of them and quite incapable of discerning priorities. During a crisis at sea, it is no use saying 'Now sit down and think this thing over carefully'. Thought has to be instant – almost instinctive. The trouble with Warms was that, unable to concentrate upon any particular point in a cocktail of chaos, he was apt to do nothing at all.

However, the unfortunate Warms was not the only target for Wilmott's displeasure. The inhabitants of the radio office, supplied to the line by the Radiomarine Corporation of America, were not merely disliked by him; they were a source of anxiety. He had a feeling – possibly no more than that – that the chief radio officer, a six-feet-two-inch tall individual with a fleshed out face named George Rogers, might be capable of more or less anything. But he was not sure of what. With more reason, he had strong doubts about the loyalty of the second radio operator, George Alagna. In his vocabulary, Alagna was a Communist. Some months previously, this young man, appalled at the quality of meals served to the crew, decided to do something about it. He prepared a petition which he circulated to the other officers and requested that they should sign it. Probably mindful of the benefits of employment at a time when it certainly did not merit the adjective 'full', they refused. But Alagna was not yet done. When the ship was about to sail from New York, he and the other junior operator went on strike. Consequently her departure was delayed for one hour and forty-five minutes. The matter was settled at last, when the Ward Line management put its signature to an agreement promising better conditions. It was never honoured: there had never been any intention to honour it, but at least it satisfied the rebellious Alagna – at any rate for the time being.

The hatchet may have been buried, but Wilmott knew that a buried hatchet can easily be disinterred. He even went so far as to fear that, in the next round of Alagna versus the Ward Line, the former might resort to sabotage.

During the *Morro Castle*'s Labor Day Cruise to Havana the outward voyage passed pleasantly enough. The ship docked on time. The passengers went ashore (some of the unaccompanied ladies escorted by the more presentable stewards – a regular happening that did little to assist the cause of discipline). Large quantities of booze were bought for small amounts of money; and a lot of people got drunk. Most of them returned to the liner with the wherewithal to maintain this alcoholically induced state of euphoria (thereby reducing the bar sales and, consequently, the stewards' tips – another situation which created another problem). Some, the more earnest and temperate, may actually have visited Morro Castle, after which the ship was named and which stands (or used to stand) guardian at the harbour entrance. On the afternoon of Wednesday 5 September, the liner set off for home. At New York, her personnel should have had twelve hours in which to scrub out, refurbish, and generally get ready for another such cruise. The Ward Line liked to keep its people busy.

So far as one can tell, only Wilmott had anything very much to worry about during the first two days or so of the return trip. Warms, to whom anxiety was commonplace, may have taken him seriously. Others might have regarded him as mildly neurotic – even, perhaps, paranoic. As so often in recent months, his fears were directed at the radio office. Word, apparently, had reached him that two bottles had been brought aboard the ship at Havana. In fact, a great many bottles had been imported into this hotel of the high seas, but their contents were merely that elevating national product of Cuba – rum. The two in question, however, were more sinister. One was believed to contain sulphuric acid – the other a fluid that has never been identified, but which smelt horribly. According to the chief radio operator, George Rogers, Wilmott called him to his cabin and asked him whether he knew anything about the matter. The wireless officer recalled the minor industrial dispute that had delayed the *Morro Castle*'s departure by one hour and forty-five minutes, and how the Ward Line had reneged on its promises. 'There was', he said, 'a lot of talk in Havana that if things didn't pan out there were ways of getting even.' However, he assured the captain that he had thrown at least one of the bottles overboard (he didn't say which: indeed, he made no mention of two). He implied that Alagna had been responsible for their presence on the ship and that, conscientious crewman that he was, he had taken appropriate action.

Wilmott then discussed the problem of the bottles (assuming that it was a problem) with Warms. The chief officer at once suggested that Alagna should be put in irons. This, Wilmott considered, was rather too drastic – but, yes, when the ship docked in New York, the recalcitrant second radio operator would be dismissed. Warms then wondered whether it might not be a sound idea if he, personally, searched Alagna's quarters. Again Wilmott demurred. The man, he reflected, was a sight too clever for that. Warms would find nothing. He should confine himself to keeping an especially sharp eye upon the imagined villain.

The fourth officer, Howard Hansen also seems to have been privy to Wilmott's misgivings. He, too, put forward the proposition that Alagna should be locked up. The captain repeated that this was not necessary. Rogers, he believed, had taken appropriate action. Perhaps he had, but there had been no witnesses; and, again, the question crops up of what, exactly, had he thrown overboard. Was it the sulphuric acid? Was it the unnamed liquid that smelt so vile? Had he, now that one came to think of it, thrown *anything* overboard? It was all one hell of a problem.

Wilmott watchers may have noticed that a change had come over the captain. His cabin door was apt to be locked. Socially, this normally gregarious and voluble character became more withdrawn.

On the night before the *Morro Castle* was due to arrive at New York, the customary farewell dinner took place. The cynosure of the occasion should have been Robert Wilmott. From his post at the captain's table, he would have exuded goodwill, remarking from time to time what a pleasure it was to sail with such charming people – and thereby possibly ensuring that he would sail with them again. But, as the festive hour approached, the news filtered through that, tonight of all nights, there would be no Wilmott. For reasons that were not entirely clear, he had decided to remain in his cabin and to have something sent up on a tray.

Whatever it was does not seem to have agreed with him. The senior ship's surgeon, Dr De Witt C. Van Zile, was summoned to what now, perhaps, merits the word 'bunker'. His captain, it seemed, was suffering from severe abdominal pains. But no, Wilmott insisted, it wasn't serious: just something he'd eaten. He would, he believed, feel more comfortable if he were given an enema. Van Zile agreed.

To add to his other worries, the weather had now taken a turn for the worse. Winds were building up to hurricane force and life on board this floating palace of delight had become a great deal less than comfortable. Wilmott was familiar with such conditions: as he not infrequently told passengers, he had steered the *Morro Castle* through just such a storm off Cape Hatteras in 1933. The radio broke down and, as a consequence, the ship was reported missing for a couple of days. But there had been no damage worth talking about. Nobody was hurt and his customers were suitably grateful. At a dinner given afterwards in his honour, they presented him with a watch. It was inscribed 'In recognition of superb seamanship through a most perilous hurricane – Sept. 13–18, '33.'

It was in connection with the present meteorological fury that, not long after the administration of the enema, Fourth Officer Hansen knocked on Wilmott's door. Receiving no reply, he went inside. To his stunned amazement, he found the captain in the bath – partially undressed and, as he put it, with 'no water in the tub'. He seemed to be unconscious. Van Zile was sent for – followed by the chief steward, the purser, the chief engineer, the first engineer, the second steward, and one of the night watchmen. It must have seemed as if nearly half the ship's company were crammed into this relatively small room. Van Zile had to inform the assembled throng that their captain was dead: that he had been dead for some time, and that the probable cause was cardiac insufficiency.

Van Zile probably knew what he was talking about, though, when she was told of her husband's death, Mrs Wilmott disagreed with him. 'I can never agree that Captain Wilmott died of heart disease due to acute indigestion,' she said. 'There is something strange about it all.'

There was indeed. For one thing, Mrs Wilmott seems to have got her facts wrong. Acute indigestion does not bring about heart attacks. The discomfort it produces has sometimes been mistaken for this very much more ominous condition, but that is quite another matter. Nor do the strange circumstances in which the captain's body was discovered appear to have been sufficiently remarked. Assuming that he was about to take a bath when he died, it is not unreasonable to suppose that he would have begun by turning on the taps and then to undress. If, at this point, his heart had given up the struggle, he would have fallen to the floor. The water would have kept on flowing until (unless somebody had intervened) it flooded the room. Alternatively, if less efficiently, he might have decided to remove his clothes before filling the bath. But, whatever his method, the possibility of his lying half clad in an empty tub seems too unlikely to be dismissed as a mere foible.

In any case, one feels bound to ask why he felt compelled to take a bath at all. With a hurricane filling its lungs in preparation for a really big blow, one might have expected him to be on the bridge – dyspepsia or no dyspepsia. And, finally, there is the timing of the tragedy. Even if you accept the proposition that life is so full of coincidence that there is really no such thing, you may find it strange that Captain Robert Wilmott departed this life at the very time when his guiding hand aboard the *Morro Castle* would most be needed.

Does this, then, point to the possibility of foul play? Does it suggest that the tray-borne dinner may have contained some sort of additive intended to get Wilmott out of the way? This must be sheer conjecture. No traces of food or drink were available for analysis, and when it might have been possible to carry out an autopsy, the captain's mortal remains were in no fit condition for any such investigation. But, by then, a great many other things had occurred, and all of them were terrible.

Wilmott died at 7.45pm ship's time. The Ward Line was informed by a radiogram notable for its brevity. It said, simply: 'Wilmott deceased 7.45pm. Acknowledge.' It was signed by Warms. Understandably, the owners wished to know rather more, and it was left to the purser, Robert Toldman, to fill in the details. He confirmed that the captain was indeed dead, and explained the cause as 'acute indigestion and heart attack' (which may have been the source of Mrs Wilmott's information. Possibly her own imagination suggested that the former had caused the latter).

The passengers were told and a kind of hush came over the ship – insofar as there can be any hush when a hurricane is getting into its stride. For a while, people seemed to tread more softly and to speak more quietly. But drink and the devil managed to overcome this subdued reverence, and those who were not stricken with the malaise that rough seas are apt to inflict, resumed their revelry. Nevertheless, a dance that was to have been the evening's highlight was cancelled.

Up on the bridge, William Warms promoted himself to captain and conveyed a message via the purser that it was now he who must be obeyed. The hours went by; New York became closer; the *Morro Castle* battled her way up the coast of New Jersey about six miles offshore. Down in the writing room, a group of kindred spirits were amusing themselves by trying to flick lighted cigarettes into the wastepaper baskets. At 2.50am ship's time, one of the gamesmen – a Brooklyn butcher named Paul Arneth – remarked that there was smoke coming from a cupboard at one end of the room. It contained 150 spare blankets and one or two other oddments, and it was locked. Mr Arneth, who appears to have been more sober than his companions, felt that it should be investigated. He informed a steward named Daniel Campbell. Mr Campbell opened the door, saw that a fire was raging inside, and very sensibly shut it again.

Meanwhile, one of the night watchmen had seen smoke emerging from a ventilator on the port side near the forward of the two funnels. He reported his discovery to Warms. In a better ordered world, Warms would already have been aware of it. Among the gadgetry in the wheelhouse was a fire detection system. It took the form of a board with a collection of red lights upon it. Each was linked to a thermostat. If the temperature of its environment exceeded 160°F, the thermostat was designed to pass on the message to its parent light, which would flash a warning signal. In theory, this would not only have given notice that a fire had broken out: it would also have revealed its location. It sounds excellent, but the installation ignored one fundamental. Fires obey no rules and they do not confine themselves to cabins. As the episode in the writing room cupboard showed, they also attack public rooms. None of those in the *Morro Castle* was netted into the system. Consequently, the lights kept their counsel to themselves until some while later – when the quartermaster noticed one of them winking an urgent signal to the effect that a cabin on A deck was ablaze.

Wilmott's refusal to do anything that might alarm the passengers now exacted its price. Nobody really knew what to do. The firefighting equipment had been badly maintained. To make matters worse, the two men that should have taken some positive action to get the blaze under control were otherwise engaged. The chief officer – i.e. Warms – was now captain and, as such, preoccupied with his duties on the bridge. The boatswain was less gainfully employed. He was dead drunk.

Poor Warms! To be in command of a ship that is fighting a hurricane, and at the same time, being consumed by fire, is not a job for which anyone in his right mind would apply. Wilmott had already confided to his wife that 'Warms is too erratic . . . He doesn't know what he's doing from one moment to the next'. The truth of this observation soon became clear. Whilst nobody could have accused him of lethargy, the fact was that he was trying to do too many things at once: doing none of them at all well, and neglecting a few fairly obvious things – such as ordering the radio room to transmit a distress signal.

Nor was the chief engineer, Eban S. Abbott, doing very much to assist him. His place, surely, was in the engine-room, but now we see him in a corner of the bridge, attired, improbably enough, in his number one uniform. The third engineer was left to cope with the situation down below – with, from time to time, visits from the first engineer. At no time did Abbott go near the place. His one concern, or so it seemed, was to get himself safely into a lifeboat.

For a while, and despite the urging of Fourth Officer (now Third Officer) Howard Hansen that he should make for the nearest beach, Warms entertained the fatuous idea that, still steaming at eighteen knots, he could reach New York. Most of his utterances to the world outside the wheelhouse were shredded by the gale and not heard by anyone. Even his instructions for countering the blaze were futile. The ship was fitted with forty-two hydrants fed by three pumps that served a single water main. Now you do not have to be a graduate in physics to work out that the more hydrants that are turned on, the less will be the pressure in each. In this case, only six of them could function at full pressure simultaneously. Open twelve of them, and the pressure dropped to one-third. Open the lot, and you were in grievous trouble. But that is precisely what Warms insisted should happen.

In the end, Warms was persuaded that his wisest course really was to go hard a port and to make for the New Jersey shore. In the end, he did instruct the radio office to transmit a distress signal, but he should have done it at least fifteen minutes earlier. Indeed, at one time, the chief radio operator, George Rogers, was in the ridiculous situation of overhearing a conversation between a freighter in the vicinity and the us Coast Guard station at Tuckerton, New Jersey. The gist of it was that the cargo vessel's captain had noticed what appeared to be a ship on fire. Did Tuckerton know anything about it? Tuckerton did not. Clearly Rogers could have interposed with the information that there certainly was one that was blazing almost from end to end, and that it was the *Morro Castle*. But the rules of the game insisted that he could not do this without authorization from the master. He had received no such authorization and he preferred to go by the book.

As it happened, his assistant, George Alagna, was at that very moment about fifty feet away in the wheelhouse, making yet another attempt to bring Warms to his senses. Five minutes later, after one more journey, he succeeded. By this time, the *Morro Castle* must have been ablaze for about forty-five minutes, starting in a smallish way and relentlessly expanding its fury.

The ship was now twenty miles south of the Scotland lightship on the southern approaches to New York. Five minutes after Rogers broadcast the signal, the entire super-structure was on fire. Warms and his officers removed them-selves to the bows of the ship; the passengers, or most of them, were huddled together on the after part. The seafarers had made the wiser choice. The wind was now blowing the flames away from them – hell bent, it seemed, for a massacre of the innocents at the blunt end.

Round about 3.25am, William Warms performed what must be regarded as his last act as master of the *Morro Castle*. By means of blasts on the foghorn, he gave the order to abandon ship. After that, he was no longer in control. The pattern that passed for a semblance of order in the liner fragmented. There were, to be sure, more than sufficient ships and aircraft in the vicinity and all of them anxious to render assistance. The tragedy was that any rescue at sea depends upon co-operation between the helpers and the helped. If a vessel is to be abandoned successfully, there must be discipline. People must know where to go, what to do, when to do it, and so on. In the *Morro Castle*, there was nothing but chaos.

There was once a tradition about the correct way in which to leave a doomed ship. The mode was set in 1852 by HMS Troopship *Birkenhead*. She was on passage from Queenstown (now Cobh) in Ireland for Algoa Bay in South Africa. On board were soldiers belonging to the 74th Highlanders – many of them accompanied by their families. They had been detailed for service as reinforcements in the Zulu War. On 26 February the *Birkenhead* struck a rock off Danger Point on the eastern side of the Cape of Good Hope. Within twenty-five minutes, she had broken in two and was sinking.

Alexander Seton, the commanding officer of the Highlanders, lined up his troops on deck. The women and children were taken off in the lifeboats, and then the horses were released – on the supposition that they might be able to swim ashore. Then, and only then, were the infantrymen allowed to break ranks and attempt to save themselves. Of those on board the ship 455 died; 193 were saved. It was tragic, but it was glorious. Kipling was just one of many who paid tribute to it ('But to stand an' be still to the Birken'ead drill is a damn tough billet to chew' et cetera).

Thus the rule of women and children first was created. In passenger liners, first class passengers received priority over the unfortunates who travelled in steerage, and the crew had no priority at all. Their job was to manage the situation: to man the lifeboats, but also to ensure that as many people as possible got into them. Since, until after the loss of the *Titanic* in 1912, there were seldom enough boats to accommodate everyone on board, this was a tough assignment. In any case, the system often collapsed due to inadequate communications.

By the time of the *Morro Castle* disaster, the tradition had lost much of its force; the 'Birkenhead spirit' (as it was called) was almost spent. In a ship such as this, with a dissatisfied crew, and a fumbler such as Warms in command, there was no pretence at heroism. The women and children had best look after themselves, for the men certainly intended to do so. The crew, in particular, demonstrated an acute sense of self-preservation. The figures speak for themselves. Out of 200 officers and crewmen, only 34 died (including Dr Van Zile). One hundred of the 321 passengers perished – in other words, about 33 per cent of the latter died and only 17 per cent of the former. About the only member of the vessel's personnel who came out of the affair with any credit was chief radio operator George Rogers. He had remained at his post, half-smothered by smoke and tortured by intense heat, until his apparatus was incapable of transmitting or receiving. Only then did he attempt to save himself.

The wind, the waves and the current had taken charge of the *Morro Castle* – or what remained of her. With a nice sense of judgement, they carried her ashore on the beach of Ashbury Park, New Jersey. The city's pier, its Convention Hall, and the broadwalk at the foot of Sunset Avenue, were all within a few yards. From a spectator's point of view this was perfect. Not long after the fire had extinguished itself and the heat had abated, touts were charging admission fees to anyone of a sufficiently ghoulish disposition that wished to explore the wreck. Prices varied, beginning at five dollars plus an extra five dollars to hire a gas mask, and eventually decreasing to twenty-five cents.

George Rogers was accorded heroic status and hired by RKO pictures to tell his story from the stage of the local Rialto Cinema. Since the rate of payment was five times that of his salary as a radio operator, he had no hesitation in accepting. His assistant, George Alagna, fared less well. Though nothing was proven at the inquiry into the disaster, the finger of suspicion pointed at him as a possible fire raiser. Had he not engineered a strike? Was not Captain Wilmott wary of him – to such an extent that he proposed to dismiss him? Might not an act of sabotage even the score in his contest with the Ward Line? In fact, his conduct had been scarcely less exemplary than that of Rogers. But it was too much. Not long afterwards, he attempted to commit suicide (unsuccessfully) in his apartment in the New York borough of Queens.

Neither William Warms nor Chief Engineer Eban Abbott received any applause for their performances: indeed so many and so various were the charges against them that they were put on trial. Warms was sentenced to two years' imprisonment for his mismanagement of the situation; Abbott to four years. On appeal, however, the judgements were reversed. The United States Circuit Court of Appeal actually went so far as to acclaim the very temporary master mariner for maintaining 'the best traditions of the sea by staying on his vessel until the bridge had burnt from under him'. No such praise was lavished on the wretched Abbott, but at least he got off.

So far as the loss of the *Morro Castle* was concerned, it was attributed to 'an act of God', which was tough on the Almighty. But, then, nobody could think of any better explanation.

It was left to author Thomas Gallagher to open the Pandora's Box. In *Fire at Sea* (1959), as fine a piece of investigative writing as ever came off a typewriter, he posed a most convincing explanation and one that, to most people, contained consider-able surprises. Mr Gallagher assiduously delved into the record of the most unlikely suspect of all: the man of the hour, the giant who remained at his post when all but he had fled – Chief Radio Officer George Rogers. The heroic Mr Rogers, the man who could inspire confidence with his charm, the undoubtedly able technician, was not quite as he appeared to be. He had originally been employed in the *Morro Castle* as second radio officer. His promotion had been achieved by carefully noticing one or two lapses on the part of his predecessor and suggesting that he should resign. He communicated his threats by means of anonymous letters, posted by an accomplice in New York when he was known to be in Cuba. The evidence contained in them seems to be small, but they achieved their end. His victim left the Ward Line and Rogers received the appointment he coveted.

Had anyone studied his record as assiduously as Mr Gallagher did, it is surely questionable whether the Radio-marine Corporation of America, the Ward Line, or any other organization, would have considered Rogers a suitable candi-date for employment. He had, for instance, claimed that his career as a radio officer dated back to the year 1912. Since he was eleven years old then, this must have seemed unlikely. But this was a matter of little importance when set against his far grosser misdeeds.

Item: in 1914, he was convicted by a juvenile court in Oakland, California, for the theft of a wireless set. He was placed on parole.

Item: in 1915, he was found guilty of an act of sodomy with a younger boy. He was committed to a school of correction. In 1917 he was given parole and allowed to accept a wireless operator's job on a ship. Two years later, he joined the us Navy – from which he was discharged for defective vision. He moved back to his birthplace, New York.

Item: he was dismissed from his job after being suspected of the theft of two 50-watt radio valves. They were valued at $300.

Item: in 1924 he was known to have committed a criminal assault on a ten-year-old boy.

Item: in 1929, the premises of the firm by which he was employed were destroyed by fire. The matter was never satisfactorily explained.

Item: in 1930, radio instruments to the value of $2,000 were stolen from an establishment in New York City. The theft was traced to Rogers. But, since he returned the items to their rightful owners, he was not prosecuted.

All these things happened before the *Morro Castle* affair. Very much worse was to follow it. Nevertheless, they would have been enough to establish the chief radio officer as a thief and a pervert. A little more delving would have sufficed to show him as a potential arsonist. He had always been interested in chemistry. More to the point, however, was his preoccupation with a small device that had been a hazard to Allied shipping during the early days of World War I. Invented by a chemist named Scheele, it consisted of a lead tube with a copper disc in the middle. Sulphuric acid was poured into one half; picric acid into the other. Both ends were then fitted with wax plugs and sealed with lead caps.

Over a period of time, the sulphuric ate through the copper disc and came into contact with the picric acid. The two chemicals reacted vigorously by bursting into flame. The heat generated by them melted the lead tube and destroyed the evidence. It also set fire to anything combustible that might be in the vicinity. The amount of time required to accomplish this process depended upon the thickness of the copper disc. Dr Scheele called them his 'cigars'.

Under the supervision of a German naval officer named Franz von Rintelen, who was living in America and using a Swiss passport, considerable quantities of Dr Scheele's cigars were surreptitiously manufactured on board German liners confined to New York harbour (they were unable to make the return passage to the Fatherland owing to the Allied blockade). Acting on information supplied by an intelligence network that Rintelen had established, the 'cigars' were smuggled on board vessels travelling to Britain with ammunition in their holds. As Patrick Beesly observed in *Room 40*, '. . . in the four short months in which he [von Rintelen] was in America he managed to create a very effective sabotage organisation which survived his own departure and was responsible for causing a great deal of damage to British ships and American property.'

Rogers knew all about this and manufacturing these very simple gadgets was well within his capacity. One of them could certainly have been responsible for the fire in the *Morro Castle*. There was other evidence, too – such as a disconnected fuel line near the radio room that had caused a spillage of gasoline on to the deck. If, then, he was responsible, could Captain Wilmott's death be attributed to him? Had the master died not of a heart attack, but by poison? As subsequent events were to show, Rogers was not too fastidious to draw the line at murder, and Wilmott's dispatch delivered the ship into the hands of a very much less able commander: somebody who would ensure, by his own inadequacy, that the fire burned brightly. There was no means of explaining this hypothesis. When the remains of Wilmott were discovered, they were burnt beyond the scope of forensic science.

But if this were the case, what was Rogers's motive? And why did he put on such a brave performance at the climax of the drama? Mr Gallagher explains this by suggesting that he was a psychopath and by the fact that it is in the nature of a pyromaniac to enjoy his own fire. This was something of his own creation: he wished to get the utmost from it.

Whether the evidence would have been sufficient to convict Rogers seems doubtful. Nevertheless, had Mr Gallagher been his prosecutor, he would have had an uncomfortable time in court.

Once the excitement and the horror of the *Morro Castle* had subsided, George Rogers moved to Bayonne, New Jersey. Surprisingly, perhaps, he decided to join the local police force and – even more surprisingly (didn't anyone look up his records?) – he was accepted. His senior officer was a Lieutenant named Vincent Doyle. Rogers made few bones about it: he intended to have Doyle's job. To speed up his prospects of promotion, he constructed an explosive package that he made sure the Lieutenant opened when he was out of the room. The object was to blast the unfortunate officer into eternity. In fact, it succeeded only in removing all the fingers from his left hand. The crime was traced to Patrolman Rogers, who was charged with attempted murder and sentenced to from twelve to twenty years imprisonment in the New Jersey State Penitentiary at Trenton.

In 1942, after serving four years, he was let out on parole upon the strict understanding that he should join one of the armed forces. As it turned out, the armed forces didn't want him. Nevertheless, he behaved himself sufficiently for the parole board to agree that a merchant ship would suffice. When the war ended, he returned to Bayonne, set up a small business dealing in war surplus radios, and enjoyed the company of his neighbours, William Hummel and his daughter Edith. Hummel, now aged eighty-three, had been employed as a printer on the *Bayonne Times*. Rogers also enriched himself to the extent of $7,500 that he borrowed from the old man. Trouble occurred in 1953, when the Hummels decided to move to Florida.

The retired printer and his daughter were clearly nervous of Rogers despite his apparently friendly attitude. Consequently, they did not press too hard for the repayment of the loan. Nevertheless, the one-time hero of the *Morro Castle* viewed their impending departure with concern and decided that the time had come to make a settlement. He accomplished the matter rather crudely by bludgeoning father and daughter to death. When he was brought to trial, it took the jury a mere three hours and twenty minutes to determine his guilt. They did, however, make the recommendation that he should be sentenced to life imprisonment rather than execution. The judge agreed. George Rogers returned to the state penitentiary with two concurrent life sentences to serve. He died there of a stroke on 10 January 1958.

Whether or not George Rogers caused the fire that destroyed the *Morro Castle* and, with the ship, 134 lives must remain a mystery. He never confessed to it and much of the evidence is circumstantial. However, the loss of this unhappy vessel accomplished one thing. It caused the fire precautions on United States' ships to be greatly improved – not only so far as the equipment and training of crews were concerned, but also in the construction of new tonnage. For that, at least, there was something on the credit side. But, on the debit side, the list was fearful.

4

The Riddle of the Gaul

The fate of a captured spy is not quite what it used to be. In days that now seem very long ago (but are not really), the secret agent who found himself under arrest could expect no help from his employers. It was no use trying to make contact with the embassy or with the local consul. The ambassador would be out and so would the consul. Whatever music had to be faced was his alone. It was part of the contract for a job that was not very well rewarded, and in which bad luck or bad management incurred a fearful penalty.

Nowadays, in the war of vituperation between east and west, espionage is a trade in which, given good fortune, its practitioners may have a market value. When, for example, Francis Gary Powers – the pilot of a high altitude reconnaissance aircraft known as the U-2 – was shot down over the Soviet town of Sverdlovsk in 1960, the outlook for Lieutenant Powers was dismal. He was sentenced to ten years in jail, which is an ordeal to be avoided by anyone who values his health and comfort. Fortunately for the incarcerated aviator, however, a Russian agent named Rudolph Abel had already spent three years in a United States prison, and was facing the prospect of a further twenty-seven years of confinement. The Russians wanted him back, just as the United States government was anxious to reclaim Powers. Very sensibly, therefore, the two powers did a swop. There have been several other examples.

Espionage in an age of high technology is no longer an occupation carried out only by individuals of not necessarily blameless character equipped with illicit radio sets. If William

Le Quex, or E. Phillips Oppenheim, or even John Buchan were alive today, he would find the situation in some respects changed beyond recognition. Lieutenant Powers was, after all, an officer in the United States Air Force flying one of its aeroplanes and going about his official business. One doubts whether he ever thought of himself as a spy. Similarly Commander Butcher of the uss *Pueblo* was not one to frequent dead-letter drops, or to hold clandestine conversations in bars. He was, he would have protested, a respectable naval officer carrying out his duties in the Far East.

Nevertheless, the *Pueblo* was stuffed with electronic gadgetry – to such an extent that even an uninformed observer would have suspected that her role in life was that of an eavesdropper. Indeed, there was little secret about this: the Pentagon classified her as 'a naval intelligence collecting auxiliary', and you can't speak fairer than that.

At 10 o'clock on the night of 22 January 1968 this 906-ton vessel was in the Sea of Japan not very far from the coast of North Korea. On board her were six officers, seventy-five enlisted men, and two civilians who were said to be concerned with oceanographic research. Probably to Commander Butcher's dismay, a North Korean patrolboat appeared out of the darkness and ordered him to heave-to. The alternative, he was informed, would be a blast of gunshot. Butcher obeyed. For the next hour, the small warship circled the spyship until she was joined by three companions. The small flotilla took up station around the intruder: together, they headed for the nearest port. Surprisingly, the *Pueblo*'s radio operator was allowed to continue transmitting until 12.32am. Then all signals ceased.

The point at issue was where, precisely, was the *Pueblo* when the North Korean navy first made contact? If the North Koreans were to be believed, she was within the twelve-mile limit of territorial waters. According to the Pentagon, however, she was twenty-five miles from the Korean coast. Thirteen miles made all the difference between a vessel going innocently about her not particularly innocent business and (as the North Koreans put it) the operations of 'an armed spyboat of a United States imperialist aggression force'.

As the recent (at the time of writing) bombing of Libya may have suggested, the United States is not given to underreacting.

What may or may not have been an error of navigation became blown up into an international incident. The case was brought before the United Nations. The American ambassador in Moscow tried to persuade the Soviet Government to intercede. Inevitably a task force equipped with the no less inevitable carrier (in this case the USS *Enterprise*) moved into a tactical position – in short and as all too often occurs, the elements capable of detonating World War III appeared to be assembling.

The situation was eventually sorted out by Commander Butcher producing what was alleged to be a confession. Somebody's face had been saved – though not poor Butcher's – and the eighty-three men of the *Pueblo* went home.

Nobody pretended that this floating box of high technology was not a spyship. The loss of the Hull trawler *Gaul*, which disappeared in February 1974, was a very different matter. So far as Her Majesty's Government was concerned, the *Gaul* was a victim of appalling weather some eighty or so miles to the north of the northernmost point of Norway. But, in her home port, there were unsettling rumours that this ship had not been devoted exclusively to fishing. If they were to be believed, she had also been trawling the air waves for secrets. Inevitably the media pounced and few stones remained unturned in the endeavours to show that this was so. There were even hypotheses that the vessel had been escorted by Russian warships to Murmansk and that her crew were held captive somewhere in the USSR.

The case of the 1,106 tons gross *Gaul* inspired a great deal of speculation, so it may be as well to begin with what is known about her. The older trawlers were what were known as side-winders – in other words, they hauled their catches on board over their sides. The *Gaul* and her contemporaries were stern-trawlers. In almost every respect, they marked a considerable advance. They had two decks. The uppermost was the trawl deck; the lower, the factory deck, where the fish were gutted and packed into freezers. The after end of the trawl deck (on which the fish were brought on board) was sloped to form a ramp. This was about thirty feet long by thirteen feet wide and extended to a point at which it was level with the stern load water line. Two doors at the top, three feet six inches high, could be closed to give some protection against the sea.

When the *Gaul* was built by Brooke Marine of Lowestoft between March 1970 and August 1972, she was named the *Ranger Castor*. In 1973 she was acquired by Hellyer Brothers, a subsidiary of British United Trawlers, and it was then that she became the *Gaul*. She was fitted with magnetic and gyro compasses, automatic steering, two radio sets, a Decca navigator, a direction finder, and a Loran navigation system. Her 2,600 brake horse power diesel engine gave her a maximum speed of 13½ knots: she carried sufficient life-saving equipment for fifty people and she could accommodate forty in very reasonable comfort. Her seakeeping qualities were good: she had given nobody any cause for complaint.

When she departed from Hull on her last voyage, she carried a crew of thirty-three commanded by Peter Nellist. Nellist's record was excellent. In March 1958 he had obtained his full Skipper's certificate at the first attempt. Since then, he had taken charge of four side-trawlers and two stern-trawlers. This was his first voyage in the *Gaul*. Like all his hands, he was a Hull man who had never lived anywhere else.

Before joining the ship in the early hours of 22 January 1974, Nellis and his crew had to report at an office at St Andrew's Docks, where a shipping master employed by Hellyer Brothers ticked off their names on a list. Friends and relatives were allowed on board the ship to say 'goodbye', but the shipping master, assisted by the *Gaul*'s mate, George Petty, had to make sure that they all came ashore before the trawler sailed. This was standard procedure – though, like many standard procedures, it didn't always work.

A few minutes before six o'clock that morning, the *Gaul* edged away from the quay. She was scarcely clear of the dock, when it transpired that the well-wishing guests had not all been accounted for. One of them, John Haywood, had remained behind. Mr Haywood was an experienced fisherman and he also happened to be unemployed. Without much ado, Nellist signed him on as a general purpose hand. Later that day, the *Gaul* stopped off Bridlington, where a man named Tracey was brought aboard as a spare hand. In view of the unexpected presence of Mr Haywood, it might have been argued that the job had already been filled. Nevertheless, Mr Tracey had been promised the work and Skipper Nellis was not in the habit of breaking his word. The complement of the *Gaul* now added up to thirty-six. The little ship gathered speed and headed away into the North Sea gloom towards the Norwegian port of Lodigen – west of Narvik and not very far from the Lofoten Islands. She arrived there four days later, on the 26th.

During the voyage, the mate, George Petty, had fallen ill. A doctor at Lodigen confirmed what Petty had suspected: he was in no fit state to endure the hard work and the not inconsiderable buffetting that lay ahead. Indeed, the sooner he was back within the cosy confines of his Hull home, the better it would be for Mr Petty. He did as he was advised. The *Gaul* made her way up this most devious of coastlines to Tromso; and, back at Hull, a replacement mate named Maurice Spurgeon embarked in an aeroplane. Mr Spurgeon was waiting on the quayside when the trawler docked on the following day.

It can, I suppose, be said that the *Gaul* departed for the fishing grounds that night – though, in these latitudes during February, the word had little meaning. It is virtually one long night, with only the hands of a clock to show the passing of time. In this instance, the hands stood at 2.30am.

Was it, one wonders, significant that, in the formal investigation into the *Gaul*'s loss, it was noted that, 'There were at that time 36 hands all told on board, all of whom were regular fishermen. There were no passengers and the Court is quite satisfied that no other personnel were aboard *Gaul* at that time.' This, surely is something that could have been safely assumed. Unless it is for reasons of commerce, such as fishing, nobody in his right mind ventures into these devilish and dark waters in the middle of winter. Was the apparently unnecessary remark intended to destroy any ideas that there might have been representatives of the Royal Navy on board: people, that is to say, who might have been interested in overhearing the Soviet navy's radio traffic in the very sensitive area of the sea near Murmansk? Was the Court trying to imply that the *Gaul* was no spyship? Like so much in the drama of the trawler's final days, it can only be a matter for conjecture.

The *Gaul* arrived at the fishing grounds on the day after she departed from Tromso. The next nine days were unremarkable. She was not alone. Somewhere in the vicinity, the *Swanella* was fishing: the *Orsino* and the *Pict* and the *Kelt* and nineteen other ships. At nine o'clock every morning, dutifully following the rule book, Skipper Nellist reported his position and the details of his catch. The signals, as those of the other trawlers in the vicinity, were transmitted to a vessel designated as the 'control ship'. From there, they were passed on to the offices of Hellyer Brothers in Hull. They were received some time between 10 am and noon. The procedure never varied: when the offices were closed for business – at weekends, for instance – a duty officer took over. He decoded the messages and, in the case of any abnormality, notified the duty trawler manager. Some skippers were more punctilious about this daily reporting than others. Nellist was exemplary. When Kenneth Madden of the *Kelt* was asked, 'Was he the sort of man you would expect to keep quiet for a period, or stick to the arrangements you had?' Mr Madden replied tersely, 'He would stick to the "sched" [schedule] . . . It was not Peter to keep off the "scheds". He was a man who would keep to the book.'

Since the little ships were working in what must surely be the unkindest waters in the world, where the hazards of wind are reinforced by the peril of icing, it was thought to be important to know the precise locations of the fleet. However, whether it achieved anything seems to be doubtful. In a report of the Committee of Inquiry into Trawler Safety, the chairman, Admiral Sir Douglas Holland-Martin, is quoted as saying, 'The value of a system of position reporting from the standpoint of safety should not be exaggerated. We know of no case where a search following a failure by a trawler to report her position saved any lives that would otherwise have been lost . . . nonetheless we think that the position reporting procedure is a useful "long stop" which will bring help to a ship in distress if all help fails.' Commercially, of course, it also gave the owners an idea of how their business in deep waters was faring.

On 7 February the *Gaul*'s position was defined as 72° 15' north 24° 50' east. This, roughly, places her due north of North Cape and well clear of the waters around Murmansk. Later that day, Mr Spurgeon called up the office in Hull directly. The gist of his conversation seems to have been a fault in the automatic steering and a request for advice from the superintendent engineer. Surprisingly, the inquiry report gives no details about this. Surely it was a matter of not inconsiderable importance. Or was the trouble remedied? When, on the 8th William Brayshaw, mate of the *Swanella*, spotted the *Gaul* lying three or four miles away, he does not appear to have noticed anything out of the ordinary. This might be explained by the dim conditions that pass for daylight at this time of the year. But Mr Brayshaw called up the *Gaul* for a chat with Maurice Spurgeon with whom he was friendly. There was no mention of a malfunction. Rather, the greater part of the conversation had to do with the weather, which was rapidly deteriorating. The *Swanella* was, as they say, already 'laid and dodging' (put more plainly, she had ceased fishing and was trying to escape the worst excesses of the gales). Spurgeon said, 'You're all right. We'll be under way shortly and we'll get out of your road. We're going to dodge more into land.' Soon afterwards, the *Gaul* turned to port and made off on a westerly course. She passed within a mile of the *Swanella*. Again, there was nothing to suggest that anything was wrong – though she could, of course, have been steered manually. According to the inquiry report, 'Mr Brayshaw said in evidence that when *Gaul* passed *Swanella* she appeared in every respect fit to encounter the weather conditions prevailing.'

Between 11.06 and 11.09am, two private telegrams from members of the crew were transmitted from the *Gaul* to Hull by way of Wick Radio. After that, there was silence. Nor, so far as anyone can tell, was the trawler ever seen again.

The gales that tore the northern ocean apart on those fearful February days and nights were almost without precedent. Mr Brayshaw, who had seen his fair share of arctic twilight and arctic fury, professed to have experienced the like only once before. The waves, so to speak, came in spasms. Said Mr Brayshaw, 'As it [the wave] was coming up, I saw this big white thing coming down on us. I had to get out of the way.' Skipper Spencer of the *Orsino* observed, 'At times there were some very high seas running, but only for short spaces of time and then it would ease off a bit . . . There were times when the seas were . . . as high as the bridge of the ship I was in command of.' And, as Ernest McCoid, mate of the *Pict*, explained, when dodging head to wind the trawler 'met a terrific sea head-on which really just stopped the ship altogether, and considerable

damage was caused to the plating on the front of the bridge.'
Despite the fact that she had stopped fishing at 2pm, the *Pict*
was hit by another massive wave one hour later. It wrenched
away her trawl and all the rest of the gear.

At its most moderate, the wind was blowing at force seven, or
(possibly) force eight – which, in all conscience is strong
enough. But then, as if the atmosphere had filled its lungs for a
massive blow, it would increase to nine, and sometimes, ten.
Heavy snow showers joined in this display of meteorological
violence, cutting visibility to nil.

As Skipper Spencer suggested, some waves were higher than
others. This, if I read the situation correctly, is because they
have a habit of piling up. When a faster wave formation
overtakes a slower one, the crests enter into a partnership to
produce a single enormous entity. When, for example, the
average height is 22 feet there is, nevertheless and as a
consequence of this unholy collaboration, a 10 per cent
possibility that a whopper of 49 feet will suddenly rage across
the scene. It will, of course, be very local – something observed
only too well by anything in its path, but unseen from even a
relatively short distance away.

On 9 February, a Saturday, David Close, the duty communications secretary, was at his desk in the Hellyer Brothers office.
Among his tasks was that of decoding signals which had been
sent in cipher and writing up a report on the broadcasts
received that morning and on the previous evening. When he
picked up the schedule relayed by the *Pict*, he noticed that the
Gaul was not among the vessels listed on it. It didn't seem to be
a matter of too great importance: some of the trawler skippers
preferred to transmit their messages independently. When
these were passed on from another coast station – Wick Radio,
for instance – there was apt to be a delay. Something, he told
himself, would probably turn up during the afternoon. At
twelve o'clock, he closed down the telex, asked for all calls to be
transferred to his house, and went home.

Late that afternoon, he telephoned the GPO in case there had
been any word from the *Gaul*. There was none. Next morning,
he phoned the telegram office at Leeds and Bradford. No: they
had heard nothing from the possibly missing trawler. He was
now becoming really anxious. A word with the superintendent

engineer established the fact that no mention of a mechanical breakdown had been received (the problems with the steering mechanism do not seem to have been referred to). The duty manager was not obtainable, and so Mr Close used his initiative. Working through Bradford and Wick Radio, he sent a SPY message. SPY stands for 'Why have you not reported your position as per company standard instructions?' It may seem to have been rather late in the day. February the ninth had passed without the usual reassurances about the *Gaul*'s welfare, and so had the tenth. Indeed, it was not until the eleventh that anything positive took place. By then it was obviously too late. Whatever happened to the *Gaul* after the *Swanella* had seen her must have been sudden and violent. Why, otherwise, were no distress signals received? There were, admittedly, three amateur radio enthusiasts who alleged that they had picked up May Day transmissions that might have been broadcast from the trawler. But this was on the ninth – one day after the *Gaul*'s disappearance. Furthermore, none of them was received on the Radio Humberside frequency – to which the ship's distress transmitter would have been tuned. Consequently it was generally felt that the reports could be discounted.

There is nothing surprising about this. The unquiet waters on the edge of the Barents Sea, when in their worst mood, give no quarter. They prefer to get their work of destruction done quickly without heed for humanity struggling for survival. And it was, you must remember, February. Any man immersed in the sea for more than a minute or two would have succumbed to hypothermia – a condition that is now thought to be a more prodigious killer than drowning.

Nevertheless, once it had been assumed that the *Gaul* was missing, the action was prompt and huge. At 9.25am on 11 February, a signal was transmitted with the prefix GZWT – the collective call sign for ships covered by the UK Trawlers Insurance Company. It read: 'To all vessels fishing North Bank, Norway – all vessels please report any contact with *Gaul* last reported fishing North Bank. Nil reports not required.' There were no reports – nil or otherwise.

The rescue co-ordination centre at Bodo (south of Narvik) was placed on full alert. RAF Nimrods from bases in the UK became involved in the hunt, and so did Orion long range patrol aircraft belonging to the Norwegian air force. The latter flew thirteen sorties, assisted by Sea King helicopters from airfields along the north-western coastline. Nor was this the sum of the matter. On the surface, Norwegian coast guard cutters took up the quest whilst, some miles to the south-west, a British naval force was steaming towards the Lofoten Islands in preparation for a NATO exercise. Among the ships was the aircraft carrier HMS *Hermes* commanded by Captain C. R. P. C. Branson RN. *Hermes* was detailed to leave the formation and to assist the search. She was accompanied by the Royal Fleet Auxiliary tanker *Tideflow*: by the frigate HMS *Mohawk*, and by the Norwegian warships HNOMS *Stavanger*, HNOMS *Trondheim*, HNOMS *Nordkappe*, HNOMS *Senja*, and by the fishery protection vessel *Andenes*. An area of 177,000 square miles was searched before, at 4pm on the 15th, the operation was called off. The conditions had been appalling. Nevertheless, in the words of the inquiry's report, '. . . it is also clear from the evidence that if any wreckage had been in the area . . . it would almost certainly have been detected'.

However, what may have been a clue did turn up three months after the *Gaul*'s disappearance. It was found by Arnt Olsen, skipper of the Norwegian fishing vessel *Rover*, eighteen miles off the Norwegian coast and a good many more from the trawler's last reported position. It was a lifebuoy with the word GAUL painted upon it. Skipper Olsen wisely decided that it might be required for forensic examination. Consequently he made no attempt to clean it, but placed it on top of a hatch and presently delivered it to the police office in Vardo. From there it was despatched to the UK. There was no doubt about its authenticity. A painter named Harold Hinchcliffe identified the lettering as his handiwork; and, if you looked at it carefully, you could see traces of the *Gaul*'s previous name, *Ranger Castor*, underneath.

Olsen's discovery became a matter of considerable dispute. The British authorities handed it over to Norman Hendey, a consultant on subjects to do with marine micro-biology. Mr Hendey commented upon the lack of deep water plankton on it – something, he concluded, that suggested it had never been far from the shore. But then he hedged his bets. This type of marine growth depends upon light for its existence. During the northern winter, which extends to April, there is no solar illumination. Thus, he observed, it *could* have been in the sea since early February. All of which left nobody very much the wiser.

In a two-part 'This Week' (now 'TV Eye') documentary on the loss of the *Gaul*, transmitted by Thames Television in October 1975, the question of this argument-provoking lifebuoy was considered in greater detail. Apparently Olsen had formed the opinion that he could not have found it had it not quite recently come up from the bottom of the sea – 900 feet deep at this point. But this, according to tests carried out by the Admiralty, was impossible. An object such as this could, perhaps, survive at a depth of 66 feet. Beneath this, it would have been crushed by the pressure of the water. The programme also drew attention to the species of plant life discovered on the lifebuoy. According to experts at Bristol University, it was a fresh water variety that could not have survived eighteen miles out at sea. Thus, said the presenter, Peter Williams, 'nine months' research has convinced us that someone has tried deliberately to conceal what really happened to the *Gaul*, by planting a lifebuoy out at sea three months after the *Gaul* disappeared'. This, he alleged, was supported by an exercise in fairly simple mathematics. If, Mr Williams asserted, it had actually been detached from the sinking trawler, it would have drifted to a position 154 miles away from the point of Mr Olsen's discovery. Had there, then, been some dirty work? Did, indeed, the *Gaul* sink at all?

But if this were the case, and if the lifebuoy really had been a decoy, who had done the planting? The implication was that it was the work of the Soviet Union. But this, surely, conflicts with the testimony of Mr Olsen. He found the object at a given co-ordinate. To have been there at that time, it must have come up from very deep waters. But this was out of the question. It had a smattering of plant life that could not have survived eighteen miles out of sea – and yet it had survived. Did, then, this Norwegian skipper of impeccable references bring it from the shore, immerse it briefly in the water, and then head for Vardo with what he claimed to be a clue?

The Thames Television programme made no such implication, and nor has anyone else. Mr Olsen's integrity has been respected – and doubtless quite rightly so. So what could have happened? The only possible conclusion is that it was dumped by a Soviet ship, or even a Soviet aircraft, and then the good ship *Rover* happened across it by chance – before the fresh water algae had been killed off. But, in such an hypothesis, why was there any such growth at all? Did the Russians take the *Gaul* so to speak alive, remove this one item of evidence, immerse it in fresh water, allow time for a spot of vegetation to form, and then take it out to sea in the belief that it would convince one and all that the *Gaul* had died of natural causes? The notion is a difficult one to accept, and one cannot help feeling that the findings of the official inquiry are preferable. But, whatever the case, this very ordinary circular object has become invested with an air of mystery.

Back in Hull, the scenario that the *Gaul* had been captured by the Russians was not without its attractions. Whatever the fate of Pete Nellist and his thirty-six crewmen, at least it offered the prospect that they might be still alive. There was one mother who refused to allow her son's name to be included on a memorial plaque to the *Gaul*. Nor did she attend a funeral service for the little ship's complement. She just could not accept the fact that they were dead.

However, one now has to ask why should the Soviet Union have taken such an interest in an obscure British trawler, one of many that fished the northern seas for cod. The waters offshore from Murmansk were littered with Russian surface ships and submarines. Nevertheless, one might have imagined that the forthcoming NATO exercise would have been sufficient to absorb their interest. Did they suspect on totally unfounded grounds that the *Gaul* might have been a spyship; a vessel that listened in to their radio signals and passed them on to the appropriate intelligence authorities? If they did, they chose uncommonly bad weather in which to make the arrest. And, having captured the trawler, having taken her under escort to (one would assume) Murmansk, why did they say nothing about it? A spyship, by definition, is crewed by spies. As other incidents had already shown, such captives can be used for bargaining. Surely thirty-six British trawlermen would have fetched something in the spy market? It has been suggested that, in view of the imminent Helsinki talks, the Russians were anxious to avoid anything that might be considered provocative. But if this was their attitude, why bother with the *Gaul* at all? If they did, their efforts were fruitless. The formal investigation took pains to stress that 'There was also some very slight hearsay evidence that *Gaul* is still afloat and is now in a foreign port. That evidence was totally unsupported by any evidence acceptable to the Court, and is rejected'.

In some circles, this opinion was attributed to governmental pressure and the proceedings were dismissed as a 'whitewashing job'. In Hull, certainly, rumours continued to abound. A pacemaker in this respect was a Hull resident named the Countess von Silvert. She seems to have been such an improbable character, that one is tempted to believe that she was written into the plot to spice it up a bit. She was, apparently, the wife of an exiled Russian nobleman. According to her story, she and her husband had been in Denmark, where they had tuned in to a Danish Radio station known as Dansk 2. Much to her amazement, she heard (or thought she heard) an announcement to the effect that a trawler named the *Gaul* had been seen under Russian escort. The story might have been more credible had the Countess spoken a word of Danish. She did not. Nor, when the matter was investigated, had Dansk 2 any record of such a report. However, the Count said that he had been round to the local police station, and that the officers there had also heard it. The only conclusion, at any rate to the Countess, was that the matter was being hushed up: that the announcement should never have been made and that all references to it had been destroyed.

Countess von Silvert's tale circulated in Hull and it had a certain poignancy about it. By some accounts, her brother was serving in the ship. A former Hull skipper told me emphatically that 'the crew were all local lads'. In any case, if she was married to a refugee from the Bolshevik revolution, might not her brother be rather old for such work? Diligently, I called directory inquiries to find whether (admittedly more than a dozen years later) they had any von Silverts in their books. They had not.

However, the 'This Week' programme rooted out evidence of a kind that two trawlers – the *Ross Illustrious* and the *Lord Nelson* – had been equipped with intercept receivers used for intelligence gathering – and that two naval officers, a captain and a commander, had been seen to go aboard each. This information was supplied by a former Royal Naval petty officer turned fisherman, who now, in his seventy-first year, was employed as a night watchman. He had, apparently, seen a 'big machine' installed in the chart room of *Ross Illustrious*. Presented with a kind of identity parade in which diagrams of electronic devices were shown, he unerringly picked out the intercept receiver (which begs the question of how, if it was so secret, were they able to show it on TV? Don't bona fide spies still have to do a little work for their livings?). With regard to the aerial, he was less certain. Professional spy ships such as the *Pueblo* are quite unmistakeable: they bristle with gadgets attached to their exteriors. Intercept receivers of the type that could be fitted inside a trawler are less demanding. Indeed, the aerial could be mistaken for a version that had been recently introduced to improve TV reception. The *Gaul* had one of these. This, of course, suggests that, if a tool of espionage can be confused with something that brings 'Coronation Street' to the Barents Sea, the opposite is equally possible. The Russians, whose trawlers traffic in intelligence as well as fish have an encyclopedic knowledge of this branch of the electronic ironmongery business. Surely they could have discerned the difference?

Still, in those awful conditions of that February day on which the *Gaul* vanished, one has to assume that mistakes were possible.

William Rogers, then Minister of State at the Ministry of Defence, refused to be interviewed about the matter – though he admitted that naval officers had been known to accompany trawler crews on their travels. The purpose, he said, was to gain sea-going experience – and, sometimes, to carry out navigational surveys. As for the owners, they denied that any of their vessels had been used for intelligence gathering.

If the Russians did capture the *Gaul*, they may have had their reasons for keeping quiet about it. After all, as it transpired, they would have savaged a perfectly innocent ship, and nobody likes to appear as a fool. But why, if this was the case, did the British Government make no protest: why was it, as has been suggested, so anxious to cover up the matter? Goodness knows, the US authorities made fuss enough about the *Pueblo*, and she was far from innocent. Was Edward Heath, then Prime

Minister, so preoccupied by a miners' strike that was plunging the nation into darkness; was he so concerned with his prospects in a General Election that was due to take place in March, that he did not wish to become involved in an international wrangle? Or was this, simply, a difference in attitude? In the case of the *Pueblo*, was America spoiling for a fight, whilst Britain in the days of *Gaul* had trouble enough without adding a shouting match with Russia to the confusion of problems?

Another theory ventured by the TV programme was that the *Gaul* had been involved in a collision with a submarine. According to an expert, such a thing was perfectly possible in such a rough sea – given the right circumstances, the turbulence could actually force one of these vessels upwards. If a surface ship happened to be in the way, that was too bad. This proposition was effectively illustrated by a list of such collisions that were known to have taken place. Indeed, one rather had the impression that, in view of the impending NATO exercise, it was difficult to move across this stretch of ocean without a Soviet submarine smashing its fin into the bottom of one's ship.

The conclusion of the formal investigation was that '*Gaul* capsized and foundered due to taking a succession of very heavy seas on her trawl deck when she was almost broadside to the sea, which initially caused her to heel over, and that she had not time to recover before a subsequent wave or waves overcame her ability to right herself. It seems likely that initially she was thrown so far over that those aboard her were unable to transmit a distress signal'. The TV programme, by implication at any rate, suggested that this was not the case, and that some more sinister force had been at work (assuming that anything *can* be more sinister than those prevailing weather conditions).

Which, then, was correct? There can never be a firm solution unless, after an interval of more than twelve years, the Russians suddenly say 'We have your trawler and her crew: you may now have them back'. But that can be discounted. I asked a retired trawler skipper for his views on the spyship theory. 'I don't believe that', he said. 'It's rubbish. The *Gaul* was what we call "dodging" – dodging the bad weather and not fishing. She was keeping her head into the wind because of the big seas.

There are very strong currents up there and the seabed shelves steeply. She was probably swamped in two minutes. There were no traces. We used to take scientists out there to watch the Soviet ships. Near the Murmansk coast, you could see them manoeuvring. They never bothered about you provided you kept out of the zone. They used to pass us regularly. No: the *Gaul* was definitely swamped. Her last position was miles away from the zone.'

The loss of this trawler brought tragedy to Hull. But it was a small one when compared to the devastation created by Iceland's victory in the cod war. Nowadays, the port's population of trawlers is less than one-fifth of what it used to be. Most of the ships have been scrapped with the exception of a few that have been retained to service oil rigs. Several of the skippers and mates have found work on oil rig supply boats – both in Britain and in the Middle East. Their crews have been less fortunate. Unemployment is a sorry fact of life in Hull. But even if there were alternative occupations available, how would these men of the sea react? How does a man who has been conditioned to big skies and big seas become reconciled to a job on land? The conditions, no matter how good, would seem claustrophobic. They are the victims of a commercial conflict more awful in its local consequences than the loss of one small ship. This, of course, is of little comfort to those who knew and loved the crew of the *Gaul*. To some of them, these vanished fishermen will forever be somewhere inside the Soviet Union. In 1981 somebody had the nice idea of sending them a Christmas card care of the Soviet Government. It was returned with a brief note that denied any knowledge of the trawler or of her complement. There was no more to be said. The *Gaul* was indeed dead.

5

The Phantoms

There is a school of thought which argues that, assuming there are haunted houses, there may equally well be haunted ships. From this rather tenuous supposition, the theme is developed to suggest that there are vessels which are apparitions in themselves. Some of these instances are easily explained (or so one might think). For example, in the latter part of the nineteenth century, a barquentine named *La Belle Rosalie* put out from Dieppe on her maiden voyage. Her destination should have been the Azores. She never arrived there: somewhere in the Atlantic she vanished. Presumably she ran into a storm and foundered with the loss of everyone on board. Since there were not yet aircraft to carry out a search, it is not surprising that no traces of the vessel were ever discovered. The sea swept them away.

However some while later *La Belle Rosalie* reappeared to at least one observer – approaching her home port and apparently preparing to dock. Despite the fact that it was quite early on a misty morning, the eyewitness was able to discern the identity of the helmsman. He was the same sailor that had steered the ship away from Dieppe on her outward passage. The barquentine edged her way closer to the shore and then faded away.

In his book *Wander Ships* (1917), Wilbur Bassett describes the scene eloquently, creating, as it were, a picture that would have done credit to one of the Impressionists. Apart from the helmsman's face, the definition is by no means sharp. Nor is the observer without significance. She was the fiancée of the young seaman stationed at the wheel. If we are to believe Mr Bassett,

74

her heart had been broken by the tragedy. From this evidence, it seems reasonable to conclude that it was a trick of the girl's imagination and hardly worth recording.

The case of the *Packet Light*, which was wrecked in the Gulf of Saint Lawrence not far from the coast of Prince Edward Island, is slightly more perplexing. On the anniversary of her loss, the ship is said to reappear. The show begins with a ball of fire approaching the shore. Gradually the shape of the vessel materialises in the middle of it, rather like a picture coming into focus. Flames are seen to blaze from her deck and spars until she becomes an inferno. Then she sinks; the light vanishes; and the brief drama is over. People, it is sometimes said, see what they want to see – but why the *Packet Light*? She was of no particular importance; just one of the sea's innumerable victims. It may seem strange that she should have been singled out for this somewhat dubious form of immortality.

According to one estimate, the Goodwin Sands off the coast of Kent have been responsible for the loss of over a thousand named ships (and many others unnamed) accounting for tens of thousands of lives. At low tide in high summer, cricket matches have been played upon them. Under less congenial conditions, the story is very different and it is not surprising to discover that, if ghosts exist, the Goodwins provide them with a stage. Among the supposed phantoms are a three-masted schooner named the *Lady Lovibond* and an American 'Liberty boat' freighter that went aground a few days before Christmas in 1946.

The *Lady Lovibond* was under the command of Captain Simon Reed when she ran on to the sands on 13 February 1748. Reed had recently married and had taken his young wife with him for what might be described as a honeymoon trip. Either this master mariner's mind was on other things – honeymoons tend to concentrate the mind on less practical matters – or else the ship was becalmed and swept on to the banks by the current. At all events, the schooner deposited herself on the Goodwins and there she remained until the weather, having taken a sudden turn for the worse, demolished her, Captain Reed and his espoused, and all her crew. Since then, she has reappeared at intervals of fifty years, re-enacting her tragedy. The illusion, it seems, is so convincing, that boats have actually put off from the shore in an attempt at rescue. As they draw near, the ship vanishes. There is nothing very strange in that: most ghost stories tend to include a disappearing act in their finales. However, it is interesting to note that, despite the fact that the late *Lady Lovibond* manifests herself only twice in every century, all the accounts of her sightings agree in every particular.

The American freighter is a more playful apparition. She was driven on to the sands by a gale and swiftly torn apart. There were no survivors. In her hauntings, she makes a play of being about to ram other ships in the vicinity. So alive is her performance, that the Ramsgate lifeboat has been called out on several occasions to investigate. But the story is always the same: the image dissolves before it can be inspected too closely.

Another occasional visitor to the Goodwins is the Canadian Pacific liner *Montrose*. This otherwise unspectacular ship had her flutter of fame (notoriety?) in 1910 after Hawley Harvey Crippen had boarded her at Antwerp with his mistress, Ethel Le Neve. Mrs Crippen, having been dosed with rather too much hyoscine, was assumed by her murderer to be still concealed in a somewhat dismembered condition beneath the cellar of 39 Hilldrop Crescent in North London.

When the *Montrose* was crossing the Atlantic to Montreal the master, Captain Henry Kendall, recognized Crippen and noted, too, the way in which he treated his companion. Miss Le Neve, inexpertly disguised as a youth, was supposed to be his son. The deception may have fooled some people, but not the sharp-eyed Captain Kendall. He noted the amorous glances, the ill-concealed holding of hands, and so on – signs of affection that are far from commonplace in father-son relationships. He radioed his suspicions to Scotland Yard, which promptly dispatched two detectives in a rather faster ship. The result was that, on arrival in the Saint Lawrence, the *Montrose* was boarded by the policemen and Crippen was arrested.

At the outbreak of World War I, the *Montrose* was berthed at Antwerp with her sister, the *Montcalm* – where, as it happened, Captain Kendall, was serving as Canadian Pacific's marine superintendent. Anxious about the approaching German army, he removed the two ships to London. There it was decided that the *Montrose* would be filled with concrete and sunk at the mouth of the Thames as a blockship.

The erstwhile liner was towed to her intended position but had not yet been scuttled, when a gale took charge. She was ripped away and thrust towards the Goodwins, where she eventually settled beyond recovery. For many years, one of her masts served as a warning to mariners.

It would be a nice thought to imagine the ghost of Crippen prowling her decks, looking perhaps for Miss Le Neve, or else eternally wishing that he had made a better job of concealing the late Mrs Crippen. But can, if one may put it like this, a ghost haunt a ghost? It seems unlikely. You can search the Goodwins in vain for any trace of this self-styled doctor (he was not a doctor at all: a patent medicine salesman might be a better description), but you might, just possibly, encounter the spectre of the *Montrose*. On two occasions (the last was in 1965), she has been seen approaching the sands – so convincingly that, again, lifeboats have been called out.

Obviously it is tempting to dismiss these stories either as works of fiction, or else as optical illusions produced by some play of light and shadow. However, an official of the Royal National Lifeboat Institution warned me against making hasty judgements. 'Who can know the mysteries of the Goodwins?' he said. 'Who can say what they have to offer? I couldn't put my hand on my heart and say "rubbish!"' He admitted that he had seen no ghost ships, but he had been a mere five years in his present appointment. Nor did he seem to have much patience with the supernatural. Nevertheless, the sands are continually moving, and you never quite know what they'll produce. Occasionally, they yield up their dead. As an example, he cited the case of a ship that had been wrecked during a storm in 1713. The vessel disappeared completely, consumed, as it were, by her adversary. Some five or six years ago, however, she surfaced – squeezed out of her grave. All the top hamper was gone, but her hull was in very reasonable condition – peopled by skeletons wearing naval uniform. As to the *Montrose* and the Liberty ship, they raised an interesting question. Any normal vessel approaching the Goodwins would be picked up on radar by HM Coastguard, but would a phantom vessel produce echoes? My instinct was to telephone HMCG at Dover and ask. But I refrained. It seemed a silly question and nobody likes to be mocked.

A rather different kettle of fish is the case of the Hudson Bay Company's *Baychimo*. During the 1920s, this not very imposing steam ship, manned by Captain John Cornwall and a crew of thirty-six, was employed in the Beaufort Sea, which is bounded by the coastline of Alaska and the Northwest Territories of Canada to the south, and by the Arctic Ocean to the north. Each trip covered 2000 miles: on the way, she called at trading posts to load furs and skins collected by Eskimo trappers.

On one of these trips, she was hemmed in by thick pack ice and assaulted by high winds. The situation was so severe that Captain Cornwall decided to heave-to and wait for conditions to improve. The shore was not very far away and it was comforting to notice some log cabins close to the water's edge. Here, Cornwall decided, was a more comfortable way of passing the night than in the rather chilly accommodation of his ship. It was easy enough to do and we must assume that the *Baychimo*'s complement enjoyed a good night's sleep. However, with the morning came a lot of anxiety. When they emerged from the shacks, they discovered that their vessel had vanished. Proof of her progress was supplied by marks in the ice: somehow, by goodness knows what method, she had forced her way out of the pack and into the clearer waters off shore. To lose a ship was bad enough; the fact that her cargo was worth something in the region of £½ million made things even worse.

Eventually a party of Eskimos turned up and informed Captain Cornwall that they had seen the *Baychimo* some miles to the west of the log cabins. Manfully, he and his thirty-six crewmen set off on foot through the snow. Sure enough, they found the missing ship. She was more or less where the Eskimos said she would be. There was also, Cornwall noted thankfully, a Hudson Bay Company's base in the vicinity. Mindful as ever of his cargo's value, he decided to bring it ashore and take it to its destination over land. He and his men spent the night at the base. Next morning, they returned to the ship – or, rather, to where she should have been. Once again, the *Baychimo* had removed herself – without, it appeared, any assistance from *homo sapiens*. She and Captain Cornwall had seen the last of each other.

But the last of the *Baychimo* had not been seen by more local residents. From time to time, she cropped up in various parts of the Beaufort Sea, unmanned but seemingly in good repair. On several occasions, Eskimos and Canadian trappers actually went on board her, helping themselves to items that had not been transported to the base. There were even attempts to salvage her. But, without fail, the ship waited until the boats had come reasonably close and then slowly turned away and steamed off into the distance.

There is no knowing how many times this strange nomad of the Beaufort Sea has been observed in one location or another. She seems to find no difficulty in negotiating ice that would have blocked the path of a much more sturdy vessel. Gales and high seas produced by them do not distress her, and she never runs out of fuel. For all I know, she may be still going about her strange business. It is, of course, possible to dismiss this as imaginative twaddle. Perhaps it is. I must confess that I have been unable to trace any of these accounts back to their original sources. Furthermore, if there was something supernatural about the *Baychimo*, why was she cast in this role? What was so special about her? In appearance, she was an undistinguished hack of the coastal trade and one has yet to hear of anything extraordinary about her working life. Could it be that, in the first instance, the ice moved during the night: she broke away from her moorings and drifted to her second rendezvous with Captain Cornwall? Might she again have broken away in the darkness, drifting until she either foundered in a rough sea, or else was grounded by the currents? In this very lonely place, whatever remained of her might not have been discovered. As for the rest, that surely could be attributed to the imagination. Once the basic materials for a myth have been gathered there are usually people ready to embellish them.

There are those who will tell you that the ghost of a nineteenth-century corvette named HMS *Eurydice* haunts the approaches to Portsmouth. If there is a jot of truth in these tales, they may be more understandable than the story of the wandering *Baychimo* – for, by all that's reasonable, the tragedy of *Eurydice* should never have happened. She has been described as 'one of the finest corvettes of her class that ever floated. She was commanded by a captain and officered by men of the highest professional experience, and with a crew young, but sufficiently trained' (*United Service Gazette*). The weather had been calm: it happened in broad daylight when she was no more than a few miles from her destination. Nevertheless, of the 320 on board her, only two survived.

HMS *Eurydice*, ten years old at the time, was used for training naval cadets. She was returning from a cruise: on the afternoon of 24 March 1878 she was approaching Spithead. There was no doubt an atmosphere of relaxation on board, which was understandable. The journey was almost done – there was the prospect of shore leave to be enjoyed and no hint of any danger to come. If the captain made a mistake (and the court-martial that considered the case denied that he did), it was that he kept in too close to the shore of the Isle of Wight. Dunnose Head loomed up on the port side and the high ground blocked out the view to the west. Consequently the storm clouds that were scudding in the direction of *Eurydice* could not be seen.

But storm clouds there were. One moment the corvette was sailing through calm water with every sail set and a fair wind to fill them. The next, she was struck by a force of extreme violence. Dense snow squalls reduced visibility to nothing, but the wind was the true culprit. Smashing into her at hurricane force, it literally pushed the *Eurydice* on to her beam ends and capsized her. Again according to the *United Service Gazette*, 'The fact is that the disaster, truly lamentable as it is, might have happened to any seaman.' Perhaps: but had the captain stood farther out to sea, he might possibly have seen the trouble coming. He might have closed the ports which let in so much water, he might have shortened sail, he might have . . . but what's the use of speculating. Three hundred and eighteen people died within a matter of a few minutes. As a contemporary poet put it:

'For there came down a squall, and the snow swept the wave
Like a white winding-sheet for a brave man's lone grave;
And with scarce time to glance a farewell at the sky,
The three hundred went down without e'en a cry.'

It may not have been great poetry, but it summed the situation up pretty well.

The idea behind the *Eurydice*'s apparition is that she is completing her unfinished voyage. In fact, she did get back to Portsmouth in the end – if not in quite the manner that her commander had intended. Working in almost impossible conditions (she lay in 45 feet of water, and the divers could go about their business only at slack tides and in very fine weather), she was eventually brought to the surface. But even then the troubles were not over. Approaching Spithead under tow, she went aground off Culver Head between Sandown and Bembridge. The Admiralty decided to call off any further attempts and ordered her to be dismantled. But Rear-Admiral Foley, who had taken charge of the operation, was not a man to be daunted by a few difficulties. He tried again and, this time, he succeeded. On 1 September, towed by the *Grinder* and with two more tugs in attendance – one on either side and with their steam pumps keeping her holds free from water – she entered Portsmouth Harbour. But, for the *Eurydice*, this was no more than a reprieve. She was considered to be beyond repair and she was broken up. In any case, it seems doubtful whether anyone would have wished to sail in a ship that had been the scene of such fearful tragedy.

It is impossible to write about ghost ships without including the *Flying Dutchman*. The rational explanation of this phenomenon is St Elmo's Fire – an electrical discharge in the atmosphere that lights up the mastheads and yardarms of ships and produces a somewhat spooky effect. The argument against it is that a glimpse of the legendary spectral ship is said to bode ill, whilst superstitious sailors used to consider St Elmo's Fire to be a good sign. Not without reason, perhaps, they were of the opinion that it foretold the end of stormy weather. On the other hand, and with less logic, they took the view that anyone whose face was illuminated by it would die within twenty-four hours.

The legend is believed to have originated in one of the Norse sagas. In this version, a Viking named Stöte has the temerity to steal a ring from one of the gods. As a punishment, he is reduced to a skeleton, clad in a blazing robe, and forced to sit on the mainmast of a dark and ghostly ship – eternally cruising the oceans.

However, in rather more recent times, the principal character has always been a Dutchman and his appearances have mostly (but not exclusively) been confined to the waters around the Cape of Good Hope. Actually, there are two Dutchmen and you may take your choice. The more commonplace is a

stubborn old rascal named Captain Vanderdecken. Vanderdecken, the story goes, was determined to put in to Cape Town
on schedule. The weather was as appalling as any weather can
be; but, despite the pleas of his passengers and crew, he refused
to take in any canvas. When one seaman tried to argue with
him, he picked up the wretched man and threw him overboard.
After all human pleas for prudence had failed, the Holy Ghost
intervened. Vanderdecken was not impressed. He picked up
his pistol and fired a shot at it. The bullet seemed to bounce off
the apparition and to return whence it had come, neatly
perforating Vanderdecken's hand. In a fury, the skipper then
tried to lash out at it. It was no use. His arm fell limply to his
side as if it were paralysed.

I do not pretend to know much about theology, but I rather
had the impression that the Holy Ghost is some kind of unseen
force. In this instance, the legend mongers seem to have taken
the word *ghost* rather too literally. It is depicted as a glamorised
unholy ghost shining with an admittedly divine brightness but
all too visible. However, there was no disputing the moral: in
the presence of any such manifestation, it is as well to show a
little respect.

The details of Vanderdecken's punishment vary. According
to one version, he was condemned to sail round the world for
ever without finding an anchorage. His only company would be
a cabin boy, strangely and rather horribly transformed into a
creature with horns on its head, the muzzle of a tiger, and with a
skin rougher than that of a dogfish. Sleep was out of the
question: if ever the captain dropped off, a sword would prod
him back into wakefulness. He would be denied all supplies of
beer and tobacco; his diet would be confined to gall (to drink)
and red-hot iron (to eat); and, since he treated his crew so
abominably, he would become the evil spirit of the seas.

Wagner in *Der Fliegende Holländer* permitted him a little
respite, when he allowed him ashore once in every seven years
in search of a woman whose love would redeem him. But that
was Wagner. As for his ship, it seems to have appeared in many
guises: sometimes as a brig, sometimes as a schooner, and
sometimes as a barque. One account describes her thus: 'She
was painted yellow. She was low in the bows with a great spring
aft, crowned by a kind of double poop, and what I could see of

the stern was almost pearshaped supposing this fruit inverted and with the stalk sliced off. She had three masts, each with a large circular top resembling a turret. Sails of the texture of cobwebs hung from her square yards'. With the possible exception of the bit about cobwebs, it was thought to be a very fair description of Henry VIII's flagship *Henry Grace à Dieu* (and no good came of her: she was accidentally destroyed by fire at Woolwich in 1553).

Whatever the weather, all accounts agree, she carries a full spread of sail: indeed, she seems to be strangely immune from the elements. When, for example, other vessels are becalmed, the *Flying Dutchman* hurries by with no trouble at all. Similarly, she can, if she wishes, sail straight into the wind. She is also, if one or two stories are to be believed, able to perform a weird trick. One moment you don't see her at all. Then, quite slowly, she begins to rise out of the water. First come the topmasts and then the rest until there she is – floating on the surface with her gun-ports open and completely dry.

The other contender for the role of *Flying Dutchman* is an apparently irascible mariner named Bernard Fokke. Captain Fokke commanded a barque. He has been described as very ugly and no less powerful. If any man was slow to obey him, he used to knock the offender into the scuppers with a blow that would have done credit to a heavyweight champion. However, it was generally conceded that he was an able navigator noted for his fast passages. On one occasion, or so the story goes, he accomplished the voyage from Batavia to Holland in ninety days.

And then, one day on passage round the Cape of Good Hope (which used to be known as the Cape of Storms), Fokke and his ship disappeared. The more commonly accepted theory was that, in his determination to make fast voyages, he had been carrying too much sail. But another, less convincing if more imaginative, notion was that Fokke had engaged himself in a pact with the devil. According to this hypothesis, he had displeased his master – who had demanded a meeting. In payment for whatever misdeed it may have been, he was condemned to voyage endlessly round the Cape – never getting anywhere. Of the two apparitions, Fokke's is the more retiring. Whilst Vanderdecken blusters on his way, Fokke permits no more than a glimpse. When anyone hails him, he simply vanishes.

By now you may have concluded that all this is a lot of nonsense, and so, perhaps, it is. However, there are a number of reported *Flying Dutchman* sightings that cannot be so easily dismissed. On one occasion, or so it is said, the *Flying Dutchman* was actually seen by no less than the Duke of York (later George V) and his elder brother the Duke of Clarence (more commonly known as Prince Eddy). Their Royal Highnesses had been appointed as midshipmen in the 4,000-ton unarmed corvette HMS *Bacchante*. After stopping briefly at Simon's Bay near Capetown, the ship set off on the long haul to Australia. At some point, 'A strange red light appeared, as if of a phantom ship all aglow, in the midst of which light the mast, spars, and sails of a brig two hundred yards distant stood out in strong relief as she came up.' The vessel was observed by the look-out on the fo'c'sle, by the officer of the watch, and by eleven others. The description is said to be the Duke of York's, though I cannot find any confirmation of this.

If this was indeed the *Flying Dutchman*, the evil spell of this eternal traveller was far from exhausted. Not long afterwards, the seaman who first spotted it fell from the fore topmast and was killed. Later, when the *Bacchante* was four hundred miles from Australia, she ran into heavy weather. One of the cutters was washed away and the corvette's rudder was jammed sideways. After the captain, Lord Charles Scott, had gone without sleep for three nights, the fault was remedied and the ship was able to make Albany on the south-western corner of Australia for more permanent repairs.

A good many years earlier, in 1835, a Mr R. M. Martin who was a passenger in a French ship fighting her way through southern latitudes, had this to write:

The wind which had been freshening during the evening, now blew a stiff gale, and we proceeded on deck. Dark and heavy clouds coursed with rapidity across the bright moon, whose lustre is so peculiar in the southern hemisphere, and we could see a distance of from eight to ten miles on the horizon.

Suddenly the second officer, a fine Marseilles sailor, who had been among the foremost in the cabin in laughing and ridiculing stories of

Flying Dutchman sightings that had been recounted, ascended the weather rigging and exclaimed, '*Voilà le volant Hollandais*'. The captain sent for his night glass and soon observed: 'It is very strange, but there is a ship bearing down on us *with all sail set*, and we dare scarcely show a pocket-handkerchief to the breeze.'

In a few minutes the stranger was visible to all on deck, her rig plainly discernible, and people on her poop; she seemed to near us with the rapidity of lightning, and apparently wished to pass under our quarter for the purpose of speaking. The captain, a resolute Bordeaux mariner, said it was quite incomprehensible and sent for a trumpet to hail an answer, when, in an instant and while we were all on the *qui vive*, the stranger totally disappeared and was seen no more.

If Vanderdecken (or was it Fokke?) was trying to make Table Bay when his peevish and stubborn pride produced his downfall, it is surely reasonable that the ghost of his ship, so adept at disguise, should haunt that section of the ocean. Nevertheless sightings have occurred in northern waters. The best account is this:

I was second mate in a large whaling steamer, the *Orkney Belle*, on a whaling cruise. When about five miles from Reykjavik, Iceland, on an evening in January 1911, the captain and I were on the bridge and a thin mist swirled over everything. Suddenly this mist thinned out, leaving the visibility easy. To our mutual horror and surprise, a sailing vessel loomed up practically head on. I rammed the helm hard aport and we seemed to escape collision by a hair's breadth.
Meantime, the captain signalled dead slow to the engine room. Then with startling suddenness old Anderson the carpenter bawled out: '*The Flying Dutchman!*'

The writer and his captain were sceptical and told 'old Anderson' that he was suffering from an overactive imagination: there was nothing to suggest that there was anything out of the ordinary about the ship. However:

As the strange vessel slid alongside within a stone's throw, we noticed with amazement that her sails were billowing, yet *there was no wind at all*. She was a replica of a barque I once saw in a naval museum – high poop and carved stern – but we could not observe her name. Meantime, practically all the crew rushed to the ship's side, some in terror, but unable to resist their curiosity. Not a soul was to be seen aboard the strange vessel, not a ripple did her bows make. Then, like a silver bell, so sweet was the tone, three bells sounded, as if from the bowels of the phantom ship, and as if in answer to a signal, the craft heeled to starboard and disappeared into the fog which was returning.

Neither the *Orkney Belle* nor the ship in which Mr Martin was travelling seem to have suffered any disastrous effects from their encounters with the supernatural. But, one has to ask, did they encounter anything at all? Were both cases instances of mass hallucinations?

In R. M. Martin's tale, the name of the ship is omitted; in that of the *Orkney Belle*, the second mate is anonymous. Do these exclusions suggest that the accounts are fabrications: the inventions of some writer who might have been better employed producing fiction? Both are related by a retired master mariner.* If the rest of his work is anything to go by, there is no reason to doubt his integrity. If, then, we accept the fact that he was quoting from manuscripts that had come into his possession, what are we to make of them? Mr Martin appears to have been a reasonably level-headed fellow, though it may seem more than a coincidence that the apparition appeared not long after the topic of the Flying Dutchman had been under discussion. As to the sighting from the whaling ship and that from HMS *Bacchante*, we have the testimony of seafarers who, one might assume, were reliable. On the other hand, and in another element, several reports of unidentified flying objects have been filed by aircraft pilots. Those who occupy themselves in deep waters are known to be superstitious – and with good reason. There is hazard enough without (in the mind, at any rate) adding to it unnecessarily. Aircrews, so far as I know, are less given to odd ideas and rituals that may, just possibly, ward off evil spells. And yet they, too, have been a prey to what some regard as illusions. In both cases, whatever the sceptic may say, there seems to be some mystery – either in the psychology of the beholders, or else in what they beheld.

The spirit of the *Flying Dutchman* had a reputation for malevolence; that of a more recently encountered ghost ship seems to be very much more kindly. During the years between the first

*R. L. Hadfield, *The Phantom Ship* (1937)

and second World Wars, one of the more interesting people on the maritime scene was a Finnish shipowner named Gustav Erikson. Whilst other people preferred to invest in the future (or, at least, the present), Mr Erikson preferred the past. As a result, there was only one steamer in his fleet, a 2,600-ton freighter that had sailed away from her builders in 1898. The rest were all sailing ships – mainly four-masted barques – that were employed in the transport of grain from Australia. There is no better account of life in these vessels than Mr Eric Newby's *The Last Grain Race*, which is still in print – and, if there is any sense in the world, will always be.

In 1936 one of Mr Erikson's ships, the *Herzogin Cecilie*, went aground on Bolt Head, Devonshire, a few hours after departing from Falmouth. Her loss reduced his tally of windjammers to twelve – among the survivors was a 2,800-ton barque *Pamir*. She was built in 1905 for service in the Chilean nitrate trade. Like her sisters, she was, after Mr Erikson's acquisition, registered at Mariehamn (now Ahvenanmaa). When the war was over, it seemed as if she had come to the end of her life – not because she was considered to be geriatric or unseaworthy, but because nobody wanted her. She and her sister, the *Passat*, were almost on their respective ways to the breakers' yards, when a group of West German shipowners granted them a reprieve. The Pamir-Passat Foundation was established with the purpose of training officers for the West German mercantile marine. The two vessels were reconditioned, fitted with auxiliary diesel engines, and returned to active life.

At the beginning of September 1957, the *Pamir* was at Buenos Aires, loading a cargo of barley for Hamburg. Her master was Captain Johann Diebitsch – her crew was made up of 35 experienced seamen and 51 officer cadets. The stevedores at the South American port were on strike and so the freight had to be put on board, not very expertly, by soldiers. Although Captain Diebitsch had amassed a lot of experience under sail, this was his first voyage in the *Pamir*.

Somewhere along the *Pamir*'s route to Europe there was what might roughly be described as an ambush. It took the form of a hurricane known as 'Carrie' (why are these evil excesses of nature always given names that recall the girl next door? One might expect something more suggestive of violence. Thor? Minerva? Mars? Something like that). In the centre of this meteorological monster, the winds were blowing at 80mph – and at gale force within a radius of 250 miles. Anyone caught by 'Carrie' would have to endure the ordeal for twelve hours before things calmed down a little bit.

The *Pamir* sailed into 'Carrie' at a point about six hundred miles to the west of the Azores. At 3.35pm GMT on the 21st, the Canadian destroyer *Crusader* radioed 'Am proceeding to latitude 35°57′N longitude 40°20′W in reply to distress signal from auxiliary training ship *Pamir*, estimated time of arrival 3.30am GMT'. But, by then, the *Pamir* had already sent her last signal. Transmitted at one minute past three, it read: 'Heavy hurricane, all sails lost, 45 deg. list, in danger of sinking.' Hurricane 'Carrie' had claimed her sacrifice. She could move on. By the 23rd, the weather had cleared considerably.

Co-ordinated by the Commander United States Forces, Azores, and with the US Coast Guard cutter *Absecon* as his representative on the spot, the search for the stricken sailing ship, or for anyone who had survived her sinking, covered nine thousand square miles. Aircraft from the United States and the Portuguese air forces were involved in it – whilst, at sea level, pretty well everything that could float took part. The number of ships varied; but, at its peak, twenty were involved. On the 22nd, the tanker *San Silvestre* spotted an empty lifeboat. The forward end had been broken off, but the port of registry's name, Lubeck, was clearly visible. The *Pamir* came from Lubeck. It was at once a good sign and a bad sign. They were at least looking in the right place; but, unless the boat had become detached from the ship and washed overboard, it suggested that the *Pamir* had sunk. By 9am GMT on the 23rd, there was still no trace of the sailing ship – nor of any survivors. It had to be presumed that she and her crew had all been lost. But the search continued.

Better news followed when the *Saxon*, on passage to Trieste, informed the *Absecon* that she had picked up a boat that had originally given refuge to ten survivors. Five of them had been swept away by the sea; the rest – three cadets, the ship's baker, and a seaman – were still alive. Two of them, it seemed, were very weak from exposure. They were all eventually transferred

Reports of sea monsters have cropped up throughout history: (above) the
legendary Kraken; (below) HMS *Daedalus* encountering a strange creature in
1848.

(Above) the *Morro Castle* mysteriously caught fire off the coast of New Jersey in September 1934. (Right) William Warms, Acting Captain at the time of the disaster, was sentenced to two years' imprisonment for his part in the tragedy. Later he was reprieved.

(Above left) The *Waratah* disappeared on her return journey from Australia to England in July 1909 leaving no clue as to her fate.

(Below left) Nineteen days after the well-founded super-tanker *Berge Istra* disappeared on a voyage from Brazil to Japan in January 1976, two survivors, discovered by a Japanese fishing boat, claimed their ship had sank following a massive explosion on board.

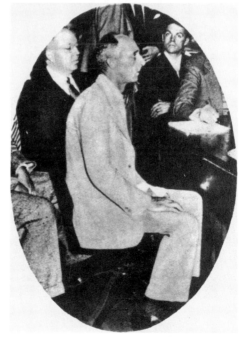

The loss of the trawler *Gaul* and her crew in February 1974 not only brought tragedy to Hull but also led to unsettling rumours that the ship might have been involved in a spying mission rather than an innocent fishing trip.

As a midshipman aboard HMS *Bacchante*, George V was reported to have seen the strange lights of the phantom ship *The Flying Dutchman*.

HMS *Hampshire* sank in June 1916 off the west coast of Orkney. Among those who perished was Field Marshal Lord Kitchener.

HMS *Erebus* and HMS *Terror* were last seen entering Lancaster Sound in July 1845. They were on an Arctic expedition, led by Sir John Franklin (left), in search of the elusive North-West Passage.

Six years after the
Derbyshire (formerly the
Liverpool Bridge, right)
disappeared on her way
to Japan in September
1980, the *Kowloon Bridge*
(below), a carrier in the
same series, came to
grief off southern
Ireland.

LUSITANIA TORPEDOED BY GERMAN PIRATE

The Daily Mirror

CERTIFIED CIRCULATION LARGER THAN ANY OTHER PICTURE PAPER IN THE WORLD

No. 3,600.   SATURDAY, MAY 8, 1915   **16 PAGES** One Halfpenny.

GIANT CUNARDER CROWDED WITH PASSENGERS CALLOUSLY SUNK WITHOUT WARNING OFF THE IRISH COAST.

1,198 passengers perished when the Cunarder *Lusitania* was sunk by the *U20* in May 1915.

The apparently harmless collier *Baralong* was in fact a Q-ship. Armed with 12-pounders and depth charges, she attacked and sank the *U27* in August 1915.

to the US naval transport *Geiger* and taken to Casablanca. The *Saxon* was instructed to keep on searching. Her master, Captain Lars Djovedt reported to his owners: 'The information received from the survivors was that the *Pamir* was in hurricane "Carrie" and that, when the wind shifted, all the canvas was carried away along with the mast. The ship started to sink, and only two lifeboats got away. The others were either smashed or set adrift. The other lifeboat that was launched has from twenty to twenty-five men in it and the lifeboat was well equipped. The survivors saw the boat next day and saw flares from it during the night. . . . The boat the survivors were in was swamped and split after the men from the *Pamir* were rescued.'

In fact, none of the masts was carried away – though it was true that the sails were reduced to such tatters that she was unable to remain head-on to the sea. Eventually, she was forced over on to her side and submerged. The other boat, with 'twenty to twenty-five' had yet to be discovered. The actual number was twenty-two. It was later found by the *Absecon* with only one man – a cadet named Gunther Hasselbach of Kiel – on board. The others (foolishly, no doubt) had seen ships in the vicinity, and had tried to swim to them. None of them succeeded. As for Cadet Hasselbach, he was said to be 'in good physical condition' after his ordeal. He was transferred to the French steamer *Antilles* and taken to San Juan in Puerto Rico.

Young Herr Hasselbach was more informative than the five already rescued – not least because the *Pamir* had not yet foundered when they left her. He, so to speak, had been in at the kill. According to a US Coast Guard spokesman: 'Further interrogation reveals that the *Pamir* was unable to keep her bow into the sea, even with the spanker [the fore-and-aft sail set on the after side of the mizen-mast – in this case, the fourth mast] set and all other sails off. Lying in a trough, she capsized and when last seen was bottom up and progressively sinking by the bow. The commanding officer of the *Pamir* ordered all crew into lifejackets five minutes prior to capsizing.'

And there the sad story of the *Pamir* ends – only to crop up again and in a very different form four years later, when she reappeared as a benevolent phantom. According to a writer named Mr C. David Simson, who communicated his findings to the magazine *Yachting Monthly*, her first manifestation took place when the Chilean sail training ship *Esmeralda* was caught by a gale in the English Channel. There the lost vessel was, apparently untroubled by the weather, exerting some sort of magnetic force which, if the *Esmeralda*'s master was to be believed, drew his ship away from the high winds and, possibly, saved her. A yachtsman named Reed Byers had a similar tale to tell. He was battling with a storm off the Virgin Islands, when the *Pamir*, acting rather like Jeeves, materialized. The windjammer (or her ghost) acted in his words as a 'tremendous energy mass' and pulled him to safety.

In her performance of good deeds, she seems to show a sense of discrimination. Not unnaturally, she tends to favour sailing ships. The US Coast Guard's *Eagle** and the present German sail trainer *Gorch Fock* received offers of help from her, and so did their Norwegian equivalent *Christian Radich*. However, there appears to have been some confusion of identity in the latter case. The Norwegian ship was addressed in German by the *Pamir*'s crew and was referred to as the *Christian Raddish*. This, presumably, was not intended as a joke. The Norwegian cadets were surprised to see that nobody on the *Pamir* seemed to be wet, which may not be important. But they did notice that one of the lads had his arm in a sling. When a survivor was told about this, he said that one of his companions had indeed been wearing a sling at the time of the tragedy. He had injured his arm in a fall on the previous day.

One question that occurs is whether the spectral *Pamir* will be able to continue these merciful errands. When she was first sighted, there seemed to be sixty or seventy people on deck. Gradually the number has diminished until, on the last encounter, there were only twenty. Eventually, one has to assume there will be none at all. It would be nice to know where they've gone (unless, of course, they are down below in the cabins). And, when the last has departed, will the *Pamir* sail on unattended, or will she, too, disappear? There are so many things we do not know.

*She used to be the *Horst Wessel* – was built in 1936 and was used as a sail training ship by Hitler's navy. Displacing 1,634 tons, she had a complement of 289, which included 200 midshipmen.

6

Enigma Variations

The death of Field Marshal Lord Kitchener (the face that launched a million young men into the cannon's mouth) on 5 June 1916 illustrates an interesting point about the art of communications. It serves to show that, if people are not informed about the truth, they will concoct their own versions of it. Or, to put it another way, ignorance is the father of rumours.

In the lunchtime editions of their evening newspapers on 6 June, Londoners read that this charismatic figure – the avenger of General Gordon, the hero of countless other engagements, and now the Secretary of State for War – had died. He had been drowned off the west coast of Orkney, when HMS *Hampshire*, an armoured cruiser that should have taken him to Russia, sank as the result of enemy action. The *Hampshire*'s complement added up to 655. There had been only a dozen survivors.

As in any other naval disaster, there was a Court of Inquiry, but the details of its proceedings were not made public until August 1926. And, even then, they did not tell the complete story. Consequently there was a large gap between what did happen and what, in the minds of many people, might have happened. As so often occurs, the conjectures were very much more dramatic than the truth. Indeed, it seemed to show that those contemporary practitioners of the spy thriller, William Le Quex, E. Phillips Oppenheim and John Buchan, did not hold the exclusive franchise. There were plenty of others who could devise reasonably convincing plots – even if they could not express them so well.

Ever since the outbreak of World War I, there had been an idea to send a top level mission to Britain's Russian ally. The government had been generous in its payments of money to the Tsarist forces: indeed, in some circles, it was hinted that it had been over munificent. After all, any benefactor in his right mind is anxious to know that his largesse has been well spent – and for whatever purpose he intended it. Kitchener himself had backed the proposal, but time went by and no such mission was dispatched. By the spring of 1916, it had become more urgent than ever. The Russians were known to be planning a summer offensive in Poland. The country was already in the throes of political unrest. If the campaign failed, Russia might sue for a separate peace, which would leave the German army free to concentrate all its might on the Western Front. This, clearly, was fraught with potential disaster.

Initially Prime Minister Asquith had intended that the Minister of Munitions, that thrusting little Welshman David Lloyd George, should lead it. But then, on 28 April, Kitchener decided that he would go. Since Kitchener mistrusted Lloyd George and Lloyd George had little affection for Kitchener, the situation had all the makings of trouble. But, on 24 April, the Sinn Fein Easter rebellion had erupted in Dublin. The fighting lasted until 1 May. Asquith decided that a politician was needed to take control of the crisis, and who better to send than Lloyd George. Consequently, the Field Marshal now had the stage to himself. He was not, however, prepared to spend too long in foreign fields – despite his eagerness to see something of Russia. Not unreasonably he suspected that, during his absence, the fiery Welsh terrier might return from Ireland and usurp him.

At one point, indeed, he very nearly abandoned the whole thing. He had agreed to depart for Petrograd (now Leningrad) on 5 June. The voyage would take six days – followed by a longish journey overland. In view of his misgivings, he was determined that the return trip must begin on 21 June and not a day later. This was all very well, but Major-General John Hanbury-Williams – the head of the British military Mission to the Russian army – had grave doubts about the possibility of achieving anything in such a comparatively short time. The matter was resolved by the Tsar, who made it clear that, however brief the encounter, he wished to meet Kitchener. Honour, if little else, was satisfied. Kitchener no longer wavered. The trip would go forward and, up at Scapa Flow, the commander-in-chief of the Grand Fleet, Admiral Sir John Jellicoe, was told to provide transport.

Jellicoe selected the armoured cruiser HMS *Hampshire*, a ship that displaced 10,850 tons, had been commissioned in 1905, and could steam at 22.25 knots. The Field Marshal had travelled in her before: in 1912, when she took him from Egypt to Malta. She would be escorted by two destroyers: a collier to replenish her stocks of coal would be sent on ahead.

But HMS *Hampshire* never reached Petrograd. Within two hours of her departure, she was settling in forty feet of water and most of those aboard her were dead.

The point at issue was: what had destroyed the cruiser? Her commanding officer, Captain Herbert Savill RN, was not given instructions about his assignment until the previous day – 4 June. His crew knew little about it, and certainly not the identity of the illustrious passenger, until the 5th. This may suggest that tight security was observed, but any such assumption would be misleading. For some while, it had been known in Petrograd and London that Kitchener was due to sail on the 5th. Whilst security in Britain was by no means as strict as it might have been, in Petrograd there was hardly any such thing. Without a doubt German agents had heard of the impending mission, its dates, and so on. Also without a doubt, they passed the information on to their employers in Berlin.

Sure enough, on the 7th – when Londoners were reading the follow-on story of the disaster in their newspapers, the people of Leipzig had only to turn to the pages of the *Leipziger Neuste Nachrichten* to find a full report (or what seemed to be) of the sinking and its principal victim. The lead story managed to imply that information about the mission had been betrayed to Germany and, by methods not very clearly described, the German admiralty had laid a crafty trap. The obituary, which appeared on another page, was surprisingly generous. It was more of a tribute, really – which may seem strange coming from a presumably hostile source.

Oddly enough, the news did not appear in other German newspapers until the next day.

The *Neuste Nachrichten* laid the foundations of the espionage trail. Kitchener's sister, Millie Parker, advanced the cause of melodrama a few stages farther. If her opinions were to be believed, her brother was still alive and well, living under cover somewhere. Or, alternatively, secret agents had succeeded in blowing up the *Hampshire*. You could choose between several identities. They might, she offered, be German; they were possibly Irish; or they could conceivably be British – the executioners of a plot devised by political opponents. As to the possibility that he might have survived, she was quick to point out that his body was never discovered.

As the years went by, the speculation did not diminish: if anything, it increased. Inevitably the IRA was brought in. In February 1916 HMS *Hampshire* had undergone a refit at Belfast, which gave ample opportunity for the mythical planting of time bombs. According to one theory, two ratings who were Irishmen had concealed such a device in the ship. They had been caught and shot, but nobody could discover the whereabouts of their handiwork. In fact, two seamen were found guilty of comparatively minor misdeeds at Belfast; but they were sent to a detention barracks and certainly not executed. Another idea came from a self-styled German agent, who (he alleged) had managed to coerce two Irish members of the crew. According to his story, he gave them the explosive devices wrapped in blankets. They concealed them in the cruiser's magazine and then, with his help, deserted. Somehow he and they eventually found their ways to Orkney where, from a room in a patently fictitious pub, they watched the ship sail from Scapa and then blow up. As Mr Donald McCormick remarks in *The Mystery of Lord Kitchener's Death* (1959), 'How three people could manage to watch from the same vantage point the departure of the cruiser and its subsequent sinking . . . is not explained. Nor can it be, if one takes even a perfunctory glance at a map.'

Yet another source propounded the notion that, at Belfast, the cruiser's strongroom was rebuilt and that, before her final voyage, it was loaded with £2 million's worth of gold – made up of United States $5 pieces. This was utter rubbish. Nevertheless, for a while, it gave the wreck a certain amount of class. There had been the *Lusitania*'s gold, there would be that of HMS

Edinburgh: for a while there was the rather more mythical '*Hampshire*'s Gold'.

We heard of British agents who were prepared to carry out suicide missions in order to destroy secret documents – the contents of which remained for ever secret. Equipped with faked passports, they somehow managed to pass themselves off as members of the *Hampshire*'s crew, and blew the whole box of tricks skyhigh. There was also the intrepid German agent who posed as a Russian liaison officer on board the cruiser. Using an electric torch, he made a signal to a U-boat in the vicinity. A torpedo was immediately dispatched: the ship exploded and this Teutonic James Bond found himself in the water. But our hero was far from finished. Holding high the torch, he flashed another signal – which enabled the submarine to rescue him.

One of the several spy stories was set in a Turkish bath near the Strand in London. The establishment seems to have been used for rather more indelicate purposes than losing weight, or the demolition of hangovers. The Special Branch is said to have been concerned about its goings on. Ten days before the loss of the *Hampshire*, a woman member of MI5 joined the staff as a receptionist. She noticed a man enter and then, fifteen minutes later, another. She recognized the first as a suspected follower of Sir Roger Casement, who was then under arrest awaiting trial. The second man was unknown to her. However any disciple of Casement had to be regarded with rather more than academic interest, and she so arranged matters that she could overhear the conversation.

The words 'Vodka', 'Big Fellow', and the 'Big Party' cropped up from time to time. It did not require very much imagination to equate 'Vodka' with Russia, 'Big Fellow' with Kitchener, and 'Big Party' with his impending trip to Petrograd. In view of the Casement connection, this seemed to suggest an Irish-inspired plot to do away with Kitchener on his way to Russia. She reported it to Sir Basil Thomson, head of MI5, who told her that it was the result of overwork and too lively an imagination. It might be better for everyone, Sir Basil suggested rather sharply, if she took a spell of leave.

Two years later, she met Sir Basil again. On this occasion, he acknowledged that her information had been of some importance, though they had not recognized it at the time. However, he doubted whether, even if they had, it would have been sufficient to have saved the Field Marshal's life.

Roger Casement, you may remember, had tried to recruit an Irish brigade in Germany – and thus to serve the nationalist cause in its struggle against Britain. The Irish expatriates showed little interest; the Germans were suspicious; and the venture was a complete failure. He was taken back to Ireland in a U-boat and arrested not long after landing on the coast of Kerry. He was tried for treason and condemned to death. It seems probable that he would have been reprieved had it not been for the production of the notorious 'Casement Diaries' – a damning self-confession of homosexuality. Public opinion was less tolerant of sexual proclivities in those days and this document was the last straw. Casement was hanged in Pentonville prison on 3 August 1916.

There have been many suggestions that the 'Casement Diaries' were forgeries; the 'Kitchener Dossier' which never got beyond an abortive attempt to sell the document to a cabinet minister, certainly was. This, too, followed the homosexual trail. However, unlike Casement, there is not a shred of evidence to suggest that Kitchener was anything of the kind. Nevertheless, like Gordon, there have been suggestions that his enjoyment of young men's company was excessive. The fact of the matter is that, on the lines of whoever is not for us must be against us, if a man was not married and did not have mistresses, then he must be homosexual. It seemed incomprehensible that muscular Christians such as Kitchener and Gordon really had no sex life at all.

As all this may have suggested, there were a number of people who wished that Kitchener would disappear; and who, when he did, shed few tears. Any grief that the politicians experienced was short-lived. Lloyd George, to take only one example, showed suitable distress – and then, a few days later, remarked that, now he was dead, 'Britain could . . . get on with the job of winning the war' (Trevor Royle, *The Kitchener Enigma*, 1985).

Nor were there any lack of theories about how it might have been accomplished. The truth, however, is much less melodramatic – as truth so often is. Nevertheless it has a peculiar interest: not of intrigue, but of ineptitude. However, before we get down to doing a hatchet job, it may be as well to remember that he set off on his unfortunate journey less than a week after the last shots had been fired in the Battle of Jutland. There were, perhaps, extenuating circumstances.

On the last complete day of Kitchener's life, he arrived at the War Office early. He spent most of the morning dealing with personal business; sometime in the middle of the afternoon, his car arrived to take him to King's Cross Station. A carriage had been put at his disposal on the night train to Edinburgh. From there, another train would take him and his suite to Thurso. Finally, another car would cover the few miles to Scrabster, the most northerly port on the UK mainland. Since he suffered abominably from seasickness, he had wanted the *Hampshire* to meet him there. But Jellicoe had demurred. He was afraid that, during the crossing, the cruiser might offer a tempting target for some prowling U-boat. Instead, he assigned a torpedo boat destroyer named the *Oak* to the task. She was a small ship, displacing only 780 tons, which had been built in 1912. Now she was attached to the commander-in-chief's flagship, HMS *Iron Duke*, for the ferry service between Scapa and Scrabster. In view of the bad weather prevailing at the time, the crossing did not seem likely to be pleasant.

There was a delay at King's Cross, when the cipher clerk employed by a Mr O'Beirne of the Foreign Office failed to turn up. Apparently he went to the wrong station. (There is some mystery about this. If we are to believe Mr McCormick in *The Mystery of Lord Kitchener's Death*, he went to Marylebone in response to a message ordering him to meet somebody named 'Colonel Datchett'. The Colonel never arrived, which was not surprising. It transpired that there was no such person. On the other hand, Mr Trevor Royle in *The Kitchener Enigma* professes that he went to London Bridge. It is hard to see how he could have expected to arrive in Edinburgh by way of London Bridge: surely he must have known better?)

Whatever the reason for the case of the absent clerk, Kitchener insisted that the express should not be delayed. O'Beirne, once he had become reunited with this man who obviously had such a poor understanding of railway timetables, should follow in a special train. The Field Marshal was not normally a patient man, and such a lapse might have produced an outbreak of irritability. But on this occasion, he was in a rare good humour. Despite the agonising prospect of a six-day sea voyage, he was greatly looking forward to the trip. Not least, it would get him away from the intrigues and jealousies of the political scene. After two years of almost continual stress, it might also provide a brief period of relaxation – no matter how difficult or contentious the Russians might prove to be.

The crossing of the Pentland Firth from Scrabster to Orkney is seldom smooth. On this occasion the little HMS *Oak* endured the worst excesses of weather, and so did those aboard her. Nevertheless, when Kitchener arrived on board HMS *Iron Duke* he had recovered sufficiently to take lunch with Jellicoe. Their conversation was mostly concerned with Jutland, which should have been a latter-day version of Trafalgar, but which wasn't. It was indecisive; the Grand Fleet's losses in terms of big ships marginally out-numbered those of the German High Seas Fleet; and Jellicoe missed the opportunity to cut off the enemy's retreat. It did, however, ensure that the pride of the German navy spent the rest of the war at its moorings. This, one imagines, was something for which to be thankful.

Jellicoe had obviously been preoccupied with which route the *Hampshire* should take once she had left Scapa Flow. There were three options:

> To steam up the eastern side of the islands.
> To travel along the Pentland Firth to a point off Cape Wrath, and then to join the main shipping route to Murmansk and Archangel (where Kitchener and his party would disembark).
> To keep fairly close in to the western coast of Hoy and the Orkney mainland.

Having cleared the islands, the *Hampshire* should have set course for a headland on the Norwegian coast some miles north of Bergen. Consequently, the eastern route would have been the most direct, and this had been Jellicoe's original choice. However, the wind was coming from the north-east at gale force strength. The minesweepers had been unable to clear a passage, and the rough seas would have made it impossible for the destroyer escort, HMS *Unity* and HMS *Victor*, to have kept pace with the cruiser.

HMS Hampshire's proposed course ---

BARENTS SEA

North Cape

ATLANTIC OCEAN

Murmansk

ARCTIC CIRCLE

R U S S I A

Archangel

NORWAY

destroyer escort to depart

Stadlandet

Petrograd

Orkney Is

NORTH SEA

BALTIC SEA

GERMANY

Inset:

10m
10Km

Hampshire sunk

MAINLAND

Scapa Flow

HOY

ORKNEY ISLANDS

pentland Firth

Scrabster
Thurso

Bound for Russia on 5 June 1916, HMS *Hampshire* sank off the west coast of Orkney with Field Marshal Lord Kitchener aboard.

On the other hand, and assuming that the wind remained in this quarter, the inshore route to the west of Orkney would be sheltered. *Unity* and *Victor* ought to be able to maintain their stations: fleet auxiliaries and coasters had used it with impunity, and the danger of submarine attack seemed to be minimal. Thus, taking one consideration with another, this seemed to be the best of an unpromising set of alternatives.

At 4pm, the wind was still hurtling in from the north-east and it was raining heavily. Kitchener bade goodbye to his host:

he and his staff embarked in the fleet drifter *Mayberry* for the short journey to HMS *Hampshire*. The two destroyers had already departed. Forty-five minutes after the Field Marshal left *Iron Duke*, the cruiser slipped her moorings and set off along the channel between Hoy and South Ronaldsay. Many of those who watched her go were surprised that she should put to sea in such dirty weather. In *Scapa Flow* by Malcolm Brown and Patricia Meehan (1968), the authors quote a Royal Marine serving in the battleship HMS *Hercules*: 'The night the *Hampshire* left Scapa seas were running high. The Flow had mountainous waves. We were shipping seas on deck and it was the dirtiest night we had seen at Scapa. Yet the *Hampshire* weighed anchor and proceeded on her journey.'

Once he had rounded the southernmost point of Hoy and joined the destroyers, Captain Savill ordered a change of course to the north. He was in for a rude surprise. At some time during the past hour or so, the gale had backed to the north-west. The islands no longer provided any shelter: the ships were struggling against a head wind of undiminished frenzy.

The most that *Unity* and *Victor* could manage under these circumstances was a speed of ten knots. The cruiser, on the other hand, was making eighteen knots. She handled badly when travelling slower: in any case, a reduction would make her a more easy prey for submarines. Savill had only one course open. With a heavy heart, he decided to dismiss his escort. The destroyers turned about and headed back to Scapa.

It was raining; the visibility was bad; the sea was in a turmoil. Battling every inch of the way, the *Hampshire* struggled northwards. At 7.45pm, she was $1\frac{1}{2}$ miles from the shore – opposite Marwick Head on the north-eastern corner of Mainland. Suddenly there was a massive explosion that tore a large hole in the warship's bottom. Immediately she began to settle, her bows dipping deep into the water and the downward path continuing. Savill's first thought was for his distinguished passenger: to get him into a boat and away from the ship. One of the survivors remembered hearing a voice calling 'Make a gangway for Lord Kitchener'. But it was no use. The lifeboats had already been smashed; and, in any case, it would have been impossible to launch them. A number of Carley floats were thrown into the sea, but they were of no avail to the Field

Marshal. Sixty-six years old, he would have succumbed to hypothermia well before he could have reached one of these potential lifesavers. He was last seen on the bridge, standing just behind Captain Savill and, by all appearances, very calm.

The cliffs here are about 300 feet high, with a mass of rocks and reefs down below. There is only one possible landing place: the Bay of Skaill. Only twelve men managed to reach it. The rest went down with the cruiser, which sank within fifteen minutes of the explosion. Up on the cliff top, a group of people had gathered. As one of them told the Court of Inquiry, '. . . some of the womenfolk were really in tears. In fact it was really a sad sight to behold, but we could do nothing about it. Very stormy night, the sea was running high and the wind was blowing down the coast.'

For some reason, the *Hampshire* was mistaken for a considerably larger vessel, a battle cruiser. This added to the confusion of a rescue operation that was, in any case, not notable for its efficiency. The Stromness lifeboat crew were told to keep out of it for this was a strictly naval matter. The mistaken identity of the ship led to a supposition in some quarters that the message must have been unauthentic: there were no battle cruisers anywhere near the place. Eventually, the armed yacht *Jason II*, the trawlers *Cambodia*, *Northward*, and *Renzo*, the former Cunard tender *Flying Kestrel*, and *Unity* and *Victor*, arrived at the disaster scene. But it was too late. They returned with several bodies and some wreckage. Kitchener's corpse was never recovered.

The newspapers told their readers no more than the Government considered they needed to know – which was very little. Kitchener might have approved of this: he had no liking for war correspondents. He seldom gave interviews. The questions had to be submitted beforehand in writing, and there was usually a condition to the effect that he should not be quoted. When Irvin S. Cobb of the *Saturday Evening Post* ignored this (in fact, he had never been told about it), he peppered his piece with Kitchener quotes. By way of retaliation, the Field Marshal denied that he had ever met Cobb.

And so, for want of evidence, the speculations abounded. Had the truth been published, the loss of the *Hampshire* tragedy might have passed into history. As things were, the spectre of it persisted for many years. On the other hand, it might have blemished the reputation of the Royal Navy. Had Jellicoe been in possession of all the facts that had been received by his shore headquarters at Longhope: had he used them to persuade Kitchener to postpone his departure until the weather improved, the cruiser might have made a safe passage to Archangel. But then, one has to ask, would the Secretary of State for War have agreed to a postponement? For him, the schedule was everything. He regarded the mission as urgent – and who knew what devious tricks his fellow ministers – Lloyd George in particular – might get up to in his absence. In his state of mind at the time, even an extra day or two away from Whitehall might have been a day or two too many.

Jellicoe selected the inshore route up the west coast of Orkney as the best of a bad bunch of options. In fact, as events proved, it was no better than the others. The tragedy is that all the evidence needed to convince him of this was to hand, and yet he never saw it. In fairness, one has to remember that the Grand Fleet had just recently returned from the biggest naval engagement of the war. *Hampshire* herself had been at Jutland, and had incurred a little damage when she rammed a U-boat (the submarine received fatal injuries). There were casualties to be counted, repairs to be put in hand, reports to be read and still more reports to be written. The fleet was not at its most composed, and one suspects that its commander-in-chief could well have done without the additional burden of transporting the Secretary of State for War to Russia. So, too, could his staff.

One omission in Jellicoe's collection of data was the Admiralty weather forecast. These predictions are by no means infallible, but this one happened to be correct. It stated that, in the late afternoon of that day, the wind would back to the north-west. Far from abating, the probability was that it would increase – reaching at times strong gale force 9. As Captain Savill discovered to his discomfort, this is exactly what happened. The high cliffs no longer afforded any shelter; indeed, from the weather angle, the eastern route would have been preferable.

The cause of the *Hampshire*'s loss was a German mine. Jellicoe assumed that the inshore route on the western side was free from such hazards. His assumption seems to have been based on the fact that shipping had used the route without any trouble. And yet it was mined – and there was evidence of the probability in some office, somewhere (possibly in the base at Longhope: it cannot have reached the *Iron Duke*).

In the early days of the war a remarkable establishment was set up in Room 40 at the Admiralty. Led by Captain Reginald ('Blinker') Hall RN, its staff included a former teacher of German at the Royal Naval College, Osborne, an ex-member of the Foreign Office, a company promoter, an art expert, an actor, and at least two schoolmasters. They had one thing in common: an almost uncanny ability to break codes and ciphers.

The inhabitants of Room 40 were fortunate at the very outset. On 25 August 1914 a small German naval force was making an armed reconnaissance of the entrance to the Gulf of Finland. Among them was a cruiser named the *Magdeburg*. She had been built at Bremen in 1912: if she really stretched herself, she could steam at 30 knots. But, on this occasion, one of her turbines was out of action and she was manned by a scratch crew. The operation was not helped when the ships ran into a belt of fog, and it was thrown into considerable disarray when the *Magdeburg* went aground on an island off the coast of Estonia. Every effort to refloat her failed. In the end, it was decided that she should be blown up – her crew and more important contents transferred to one of the escorting destroyers.

Fog, which had been the villain in the first place, now performed its second act of treachery. It lifted just as two Russian cruisers steamed into view and opened fire. This was the cue for almost total chaos. The explosives in the *Magdeburg* were badly placed and detonated too soon. They did more damage to the crew than to the ship. Nor were the confidential documents disposed of properly. One of them, it seems, was in the hands of a petty officer when he was flung into the sea by blast and killed. Next day, or so the story goes, his body, still clutching it, was recovered by one of the Russian warships. One writes 'or so the story goes' for there are doubts about this. According to Patrick Beesly in *Room 40* (1982), it is now 'in the Public Record Office in London and it shows no sign of immersion in the salt waters of the Baltic'.

Whatever the true situation, the Russian cruiser's discovery was of untold value. Contained within the document were the German navy's code-book and its key. Codes, of course, can be changed, but when the Russians very decently agreed to hand it over to the British Admiralty, it ensured that the Room 40 project would get off to a good start. The only condition was that the Royal Navy should come and collect it, which was not asking a great deal. The task was carried out by HMS *Theseus*, an ancient protected cruiser of 1894 vintage.

Intercepting German radio signals (and the Germans were very voluble on the air) produced few difficulties. Even with the acquisition of the *Magdeburg*'s treasure trove, deciphering them was harder. But Captain Hall and his team of intellectuals managed it. By June 1916, to mention only one example, they knew the precise locations of the entire U-boat fleet. In some instances, they were even privy to what type of vessel was where: even, indeed, to the name of its commanding officer.

When Kitchener was enjoying his luncheon with Jellicoe, the U-boat deployments around the north of Britain fell roughly into three groups. One was off the Firth of Forth; another off the Moray Forth (threatening the approaches to the naval base at Invergordon); and the third was in the area of the Orkneys. Among the vessels in the last of these were three ocean-going mine-layers of a new design.

Particularly relevant to this story is the *U-75*: a mine-laying submarine that had only recently come off the slipway. On 24 May, she was lying off Sylt, one of the North Friesian Islands, awaiting orders. That day, the commanding officer, Kurt Beitzen, received instructions to proceed to the Orkneys and to lay his mines off the west coast of the islands. Beitzen did his masters' bidding. Each mine was moored at a depth of thirty feet: a depth that was unlikely to bother small coasters, which might escape the attention of the sweepers, but which would be fatal to a larger ship such as the *Hampshire*.

All this was known to the men in Room 40, who passed the information on to Longhope where it seems to have remained. And so, come to that, does a signal from a trawler, received at 2.40pm and repeated at 5.15pm, reporting a U-boat to the north-east of Cape Wrath and travelling on a westerly course. The vessel in question was almost certainly the *U-75*.

It may be tempting to assume that, once the German admiralty had received news of Kitchener's proposed mission to Russia (which it almost certainly did – even to the date of his departure) it dispatched the *U-75* to block the remaining passage away from the Orkneys. But this is not a satisfactory assumption. Nobody could have foreseen a fortnight ahead of the event what the weather would be. It was, after all, June – a time of year when one expects (wrongly sometimes) the conditions to be more moderate. Had they been, the eastern channel would have been swept and there would have been no danger. After all, Jellicoe's choice of route was something of a last minute decision and something that, if all the data had been at his disposal, he might have changed even then. The options were open until the very moment when the *Hampshire* steamed out of Scapa Flow.

As things turned out, the commander-in-chief having settled the question of the route, had another problem on his mind. The question was whether, once the *Hampshire* had deposited the Field Marshal and his party at Archangel, she should return to Scapa and then make another trip to collect him – or whether she should remain at the Russian port throughout his stay. Having made up his mind, Jellicoe then had to seek Admiralty approval. At 7.35pm, Captain Savill received a signal telling him to remain at Archangel. It had to be acknowledged. It was. This was the last communication ever received from the cruiser and her commanding officer.

Neither the *U-75* nor her captain survived the war. Ironically, perhaps, the submarine herself fell victim to a mine off Terschilling in 1917. Commander Beitzen, now in command of the *U-102*, survived for a little bit longer – until his boat, too, struck a mine in the North Sea one day in September 1918. The avenger Kitchener was himself avenged, but the stories multiplied. One theory after another was propounded, and the *Hampshire* was not allowed to lie quietly in her grave. The last piece of evidence was put into place during two visits to the wreck, in 1977 and 1983, by the American film producer John R. Breckenridge. He found the ship in a surprisingly good state of preservation. He also observed that the plates were bent *inward* at the bows. In other words, the explosion must have come from an external source. The case against time bombs and other forms of skullduggery was complete. The mystery was solved – assuming there ever was one. Had all the facts been presented at the time, or even immediately after the war, there would have been no sinister suggestions: just a sorry tale of blunder.

Nowadays, a stone tower on Marwick Head commemorates the loss of HMS *Hampshire*. It was paid for entirely by the islanders. The Government did not contribute a penny.

7

Icebound

One day in the late July of 1845, the whaler *Enterprise*, commanded by Captain Martin, was moored to an iceberg at the entrance to Lancaster Sound – that ice-infested waterway that is the eastern key to the secrets of northernmost Canada. The mainland of the North American continent lies on the southern side of it: on the other, a huge archipelago. Anyone who ventures beyond this haphazard scattering of islands will, if he is on the right course and has the stamina of a giant, eventually arrive at the north pole.

It was a fine day at the time of year when the sun never quits the sky. There are, admittedly, many times when it cannot be seen. But, above the cloud mass, it is there. Even nowadays, shipping is a rarity in the Lancaster Sound. In 1845, the chances of encountering another vessel were very unlikely indeed. Nevertheless, on that July day, the *Enterprise* was treated to the sight of two warships flying the white ensign and sailing in close formation. They were much alike: each registering about 370 tons, barque-rigged, and fitted with a small funnel not unlike the chimney of a railway locomotive. In battle they were designed to be used as bomb ships, but no wars were being fought in this lonely, utterly desolate, part of the world. What, then, was their purpose? Captain Martin was eager to know. As the ships drew closer, he hailed them.

During the conversation that followed, it transpired that one was HMS *Erebus*; the other, slightly smaller, HMS *Terror*. They were manned by a total of 139 officers and men and carried sufficient food to last for three years. The overall commander was a 59-year-old naval officer, Captain Sir John Franklin. As Sir John explained, the object was exploration. If everything went as he had planned, they would discover the North-West Passage: a sea route that, assuming it existed, would link the Atlantic with the Pacific and provide a short cut from Europe to the Far East.

Captain Martin may well have been sceptical. For centuries men had been seeking this elusive channel. Some had died in the quest; none had found it. And, even if Sir John were more fortunate than his predecessors, what good would it do? For much of the year, this region at the top of the world was covered with ice. Even in summer, clusters of bergs might bar the way. The use of any such passage would, at best, be a seasonable business. However, he was not one to scorn such an enterprise. He wished Sir John and his band of intrepid mariners well and watched the two ships as they entered the Sound. It was the last that anyone other than an Eskimo or two saw of HMS *Erebus* and HMS *Terror*; the last that anyone aboard them saw of what might have passed for the outside world.

Ever since the sixteenth century, navigators had been looking for a short sea route to the Orient: something that, as it were, would bring those rich lands with their lavish exports a little closer. There had been innumerable expeditions, but every one of them had failed. In 1380 a Venetian named Niccolo Zeno had drawn a map of what he thought this northerly part of the new world might be like. There were, to be fair, one or two features that were accurate, but the rest was imagination. His reasoning was based on the medieval theory that all the land masses of the world were linked together. Iceland and Greenland, for example, couldn't possibly be two entirely separate islands. To rectify this error on the part of creation, Zeno invented a country that he named Friesland, which occupied the space in between.

Most of us are dreamers and we all play guessing games in our minds. No harm can come of it provided the results of our fantasies are not taken too seriously. The trouble in Zeno's case came many years after his death – in 1558. Two brothers who were descended from him came across his handiwork, assumed it to be an important contribution to geography, and published it. As a consequence, for the better part of 200 years, this entirely spurious view of the earth's north-west corner was assumed to be the truth. It might have been better if the whole work had been fiction, but there was just enough fact in it to make it convincing.

For example when, in 1576, Sir Martin Frobisher set off in search of the North-West Passage, he was amazed at how closely the reality of the Greenland coast accorded with the Zeno concept of it. But Sir Martin, perhaps, was rather too gullible. For his first voyage into the unexplored region north of the Arctic Circle, he took two ships (the *Gabriel* and the *Michael*) and a ten-foot pinnace. He made a landfall to the south-east of Baffin Island (at the entrance to the Hudson Strait) and then ran into a storm. The little pinnace foundered with all her hands; the captain of the *Michael* had second thoughts about the project and returned to England. But Sir Martin was made of sterner stuff. He took the *Gabriel* sixty miles up the strait and then went ashore. To his amazement and delight he came across rock that, so far as he could tell, was rich with gold.

Like many another early explorer, he was something of an opportunist. The quest for a short cut to Cathay and all the rest of the Orient might have eluded him, but he had come across wealth beyond his wildest imaginings. This was indeed something to be exploited. This obscure, unmapped part of the world was certainly worth another visit.

He made two more voyages: the first to formulate plans to establish gold mines, the second to fulfil them. His idea was to establish a settlement of about one hundred men. He gathered together fifteen ships. One of them was loaded with a kind of prefabricated building that would, he assumed, provide sufficient shelter until rather more permanent residences could be established. But it was as if this unkind quarter of the globe was resentful of intruders. An awful storm blew up. The convoy was scattered and most of the vessels were sunk. Whether by good seamanship or by good luck, Sir Martin survived. He returned to his apparently gold rich place, and loaded his ship with sufficient rocks to raise the blood pressure of any latterday insurance underwriter.

Heaven possibly knows what dreams of avarice he enjoyed as he struggled back across the Atlantic. But then reality, as it has such an unfortunate habit of doing, demolished them. Viewed by more expert eyes, the rocks were found to contain no trace of gold whatsoever. The enterprise had been a most terrible waste of lives and money. He would have been better employed plundering Spanish ships on the West Indies route: a task to which he returned with considerable zeal.

The Hudson Strait, in any case, was a false clue for anyone seriously looking for a North-West Passage. It leads to Hudson Bay and that is just about that. A very considerable victim of the trap was the man after whom it is named: Henry Hudson. In 1610 this redoubtable explorer – now aged sixty –set off in search of the elusive passage. He sailed his ship (the *Discovery*) up the strait and then, quite wrongly, headed south. Eventually after a longish voyage down what he described as this 'great and whirling sea', he reached James Bay at its southern extremity. Here, he decided, would be a suitably sheltered place in which to pass the winter.

If hell, in its traditional form, must be considered hot, this was quite another version. Nevertheless, the excesses of discomfort qualified it for inclusion in any list of places where one would rather not be. By the following spring, his crew had endured enough. Somebody else might take up the quest for the possibly imaginary shipping lane: so far as the sailors were concerned, they proposed to return to England. When Hudson tried to convince them of the rightness of his cause and his execution of it, they mutinied. The elderly explorer, his son, and eight seamen who had remained loyal to him, were set adrift in a boat. They presumably died of exposure. Then the remainder prepared the *Discovery* to return whence she had come.

Justice of two kinds was in store for them. Normally, the Eskimos were the most friendly of people. When, for example, John Davis explored the west coast of Greenland in 1586, he took with him a party of musicians. With their assistance, his sailors put on a song and dance act, which delighted the local inhabitants. In the case of the *Discovery*'s crew, however, things were very different. With uncanny perspicacity, the Eskimos murdered the ringleaders of the mutiny – and the others were lucky to get away. When, at last, the survivors reached England, they were clapped into gaol.

Until the end of the Napoleonic Wars, the quest for a North-

West Passage had been largely sponsored by commerce. But now, with a considerable fleet on its hands and no hostilities to engage the men and the ships, the Admiralty began to take an interest. Such men as Parry, Ross, and other great names of the Arctic were dispatched to look for it. They filled in several parts of the map of northern Canada, but failed to join the Atlantic to the Pacific. The great initiator of these expeditions was the Secretary of the Admiralty, John Barrow. Barrow was a Liverpudlian: born, as they say, of humble parents, whose drive and initiative (again as they say) had brought him high office. He was much travelled; had been a founder member of the Royal Geographical Society, an early contributor to the *Encyclopaedia Britannica*, and a man with a consuming passion for Arctic exploration. He never actually went to these unkindly places, but that did not deter him from writing *Voyages of Discovery and Research in the Arctic Regions*. Nor did it diminish the zeal with which he dispatched others to them – to such an extent that he became known as 'the father of British Arctic exploration'.

Barrow was much concerned that a North-West Passage should be discovered. It was doubtless due to his suggestion that an Act of Parliament, passed in 1818, promised substantial rewards to anyone who might find it. As time went on, his enthusiasm quickened. Clearly he was inspired by a spirit of curiosity. No less surely, he was convinced that such a route would be beneficial to British trade. But he was also prompted by a factor that would be familiar to any present day American: the fear that Russia might get there first.

The far northern regions of Canada remained obdurate in refusing to disclose their secret. In 1828 Parliament repealed its act offering financial gains to the brave, the strong and the utterly determined. But none of this reduced Barrow's ardour. As he pointed out, there was yet another benefit to be had from such explorations. The location of the northern magnetic pole had been discovered by James Ross in 1836. If more could be discovered about this mysterious force, it would surely improve the not very exact science of navigation.

In 1844 he submitted yet another scheme to their lordships at the Admiralty. He was now eighty years old, and yet his enthusiasm showed no signs of flagging. It might, he rather wildly suggested, be achieved in twelve months. Whether his masters seriously believed this must be doubtful. Nevertheless, if a mite reluctantly, they agreed. After all, Barrow was due to retire in the following year. Then, perhaps, the Arctic and themselves might be left in peace.

Expeditions require leaders, and one name that was constantly cropping up was that of Sir John Franklin. Sir John was now fifty-nine, and Barrow would have preferred a younger candidate. But he had already been up in these regions on two occasions and had experienced their worst excesses. As one of his officers, Lieutenant Irving RN, wrote, 'We are commanded by a fine old fellow of whom you may have read, I daresay, eating his boots'. Furthermore, there was a strong Franklin lobby. Sir Edward Parry, who had, himself, sought the Passage, said 'He is a fitter man for the job than any I know. If you don't let him go, the man will die of disappointment.' The possibility of Franklin's death from a broken heart may not have been the best of reasons for his preferment; but 'fitter', perhaps, carried some kind of conviction. Lady Franklin, seldom at a loss for a word, was no less forthright – if again for the wrong reason. 'I dread exceedingly', she said, 'the effect on his mind of being without honourable and immediate employment.' No doubt the wives of many men approaching the age of retirement have, and have had, similar misgivings. Usually the remedy turns out to be golf, but Franklin wasn't that kind of man.

John Franklin had served at the Battle of Copenhagen as a midshipman in HMS *Polyphemus* and at Trafalgar as signal officer in HMS *Bellerophon*. In 1818 he had commanded HMS *Trent* which, with three other ships under the overall command of Captain David Buchan, had surveyed thousands of miles along the North American coastline and had paid more than a cursory visit to the Mackenzie River. In 1825 he returned to the North-West Territory and did not come back until 1827. If Lieutenant Irving is to be believed, he must have accustomed his system to a diet of boiled boots, although conditions on the second expedition were not quite so dreadful as on the first. The nation showed its gratitude for his questing spirit, his ability to avoid frostbite and scurvy, by conferring a knighthood upon him in 1829. Seven years later, he was appointed Governor of Tasmania.

Accounts of his experiences in these very much more comfortable surroundings vary. On the one hand, he appears to have had a good influence upon the convicts. On the other, he may have been less successful in his dealings with the more law-abiding settlers. At all events, when he returned to the UK in 1843, his reputation had lost some of its lustre. But this may have been due to his second wife, Jane – who naturally took it upon herself to rule Tasmanian social life, and may have been less than tactful in her execution of the task. Whether his first wife, Eleanor Porden, would have been more successful seems to be doubtful. The former Miss Porden was a poet who wrote in the romantic idiom and was a force with which to be reckoned in a literary splinter group known as 'The Clouds'. One of her works, 'An Esquimaux Girl's Lament', was dedicated to Sir John before he achieved his title. Somehow one doesn't see her transcendental outlook captivating Tasmanian society of the nineteenth century, but one may be wrong.

Whatever the reason, not the least of Sir John's motives for wishing to lead Barrow's proposed expedition was to restore his image. Another was that, in view of his age, this was his last chance of a sea-going appointment. When his name was submitted to the First Lord of the Admiralty, Lord Haddington, his lordship made no objections, and Barrow evidently overcame his own misgivings about the matter of age. But, then, neither of the two ships set aside for the venture were in the first flush of her youth. HMS *Erebus*, a bomb ketch of 372 tons, had been launched in 1826; the 326 tons *Terror* was even older – dating back to 1813. However, both had given good accounts of themselves on James Ross's journeys in the Antarctic from 1839 to 1843. Now it was hard to imagine one without the other – just as there can surely be no *Scharnhorst* without a *Gneisenau*, or (come to that) a Marks without a Spencer.

For the purposes of Franklin's exploration, the two were taken to Woolwich Dockyard, where they were given a thorough overhaul. Their bows were strengthened against the impact of ice by the addition of sheet iron. A hot water system was installed with the idea of making the cabins warmer; and two 20hp steam engines, each originally intended for a railway locomotive, were fitted – one to *Erebus*, the other to *Terror*.

Propulsion, in both cases, was by means of a screw that could be raised to avoid damage from ice.

We are indebted to Lieutenant Irving for a rather more colourful description. 'We tried our screws [he wrote] and went *four* miles an hour. Our engine once ran somewhat faster on the Birmingham line . . . It has a funnel the same size and height as it had on the railway, and makes the same dreadful puffings and screamings, and will astonish the Esquimaux not a little.' The fact that it was possible to carry no more than twelve days' supply of coal suggests that its use was likely to be infrequent. Indeed, Irving himself stressed that '. . . it will never be used when we can make any progress at all by other means'.

Franklin proposed to sail in *Erebus* with Captain James Fitzjames as second-in-command. *Terror* was to be commanded by Captain Francis Crozier, who was also Franklin's deputy. All this reflects great credit on Fitzjames who, in Barrow's mind, had been chosen to lead the expedition. He seems to have taken his replacement – not only as overall commander, but also as the next in line – with singularly good grace.

Despite Barrow's suggestion that the matter might be accomplished in as little as a year, enough food to last for three years was put on board. Nor was there any lack of materials for the men's recreational needs. Sir John Franklin was a man who had a considerable concern for the spiritual welfare of those who served under him – and, indeed, for their education. He took the trouble to ensure that there were plenty of pens and ample paper, slates and arithmetic books, to while away the endless winter nights improvingly. Each ship had a library of 1,200 books among which you could find Dickens, back numbers of *Punch*, and, for the more technically minded, good solid stuff about the workings of steam engines. Each, too, had a hand organ with a sufficient supply of music (in *A History of Polar Exploration*, Mr L. P. Kirwan notes that, of the fifty tunes available, ten were psalms or hymns).

With so much concern (and quite rightly, too) spent on the physical and intellectual diet of the men, it may seem strange that less attention was paid to their clothing. They were, admittedly, issued with warm underwear and there were a few wolfskin blankets available. Apart from this, writes Mr Kirwan, 'the Arctic clothing of the Franklin expedition was the stout blue cloth of Her Majesty's Navy'. Surely, with so much experience of these icy latitudes, he must have realized that what will serve for Spithead is less satisfactory several hundred miles north of the Arctic Circle? As for the Admiralty, it may have argued that what had been sufficient already would suffice again – just as it took no trouble to have a relief expedition prepared. It pointed out that no Arctic venture of the Royal Navy had yet met with a major disaster, so why should it on this occasion? Such assumptions are as dangerous as not touching wood.

There was, indeed, only one doubter and he was treated with the contempt that he appeared to deserve. His name was Dr Richard King – a physician who had trained at Guy's and St Thomas's, and who had been involved in the successful search when Ross went missing in 1833. Dr King told Franklin that he didn't believe any expedition by sea would discover the passage – not least because nobody yet knew sufficient about the lands of the Arctic. Furthermore, King was sceptical of exploring sailors. He believed that they passed the time in winter 'acting plays and other merry Andrew tricks'. Maybe; but not if they were Franklin's men. He had more mind-improving activities to offer them.

But Dr King's warnings were unheeded. In May 1845 HMS *Erebus* and HMS *Terror* sailed from Greenhithe on the Thames. Three weeks later, they called at Stromness on the west coast of Orkney; and, three weeks after that, at Disko in western Greenland, where a large glacier meets the sea and manufactures icebergs. On 13 July the two ships sailed from this lonely trading post – towards their brief encounter with the whaler *Enterprise*. By all accounts, everything was going well. The weather was tolerably good; Dr Goodsir, employed in the *Erebus* as assistant surgeon, had done some remarkable work by bringing to the surface creatures not normally found at a depth of less than eighteen hundred feet; and the morale of both ships' crews was good.

Despite Barrow's notion, nobody really expected the vessels to return to England before 1847. But when they did get back, and public opinion was in no doubt about this, the men and the ships should receive the treatment reserved for conquering heroes. What better tribute could there be, somebody suggested, than that *Erebus* and *Terror* should be taken to Portsmouth and moored alongside that greatest of naval memorials, HMS *Victory*. It was a nice idea; but, as the year progressed and the masts of neither the one nor the other were sighted, people began to worry. Had something gone wrong? Surely they should be back by now? And then (later) why didn't the Admiralty do something about it? The top brass had already dismissed the idea of a relief expedition as 'an absurdity'. Now, when James Ross brought up the matter, their lordships pointed out that Her Majesty's Navy had other things to do with Her Majesty's ships. The Hudson's Bay Company had whalers and trading posts in the North-West Territory. It could be relied upon to do whatever was necessary.

Trying to sort out the attempts to discover what had become of Franklin, his men and his ships, is rather like unravelling a skein of wool that has been attacked by a singularly industrious cat. According to most estimates, there were no fewer than thirty-nine expeditions over a period of ten years. Six of them were made overland; at one time, fifteen vessels were deployed simultaneously. On the other hand (if you'll forgive this mixture of metaphors), several of them were like branches stemming from a single tree.

Sir John Ross, a veteran of the Arctic who was now aged seventy, began the outcry by telling the Admiralty that he had pledged himself to Franklin – saying that, if his friend hadn't returned by 1847, he would personally lead a search party. His nephew, James Ross, agreed that he had heard some such talk, but had dismissed it as 'an absurd proposition'. Others were even more unkind. They attributed it to the vanity of an old man who wished to make a come-back. As for the Admiralty, it stated that there was no cause for anxiety and perhaps they'd consider some action in the following year.

To his credit, John Barrow – now retired and ennobled by the customary knighthood – recalled that the Franklin venture had been his idea and that it was surely incumbent upon him to use whatever influence he had left. Four months after John Ross's submission had been turned down, he produced a plan. The gist of it was that two ships should be employed in a kind of pincer movement. One would make its approach from the

Bering Strait and grope eastwards; the other would enter from the east by way of Lancaster Sound. The latter would follow the route that Franklin was thought to have taken: through Lancaster Sound to Barrow Strait, and thence to the south of Banks Island (believed to be small) and into the Bering Strait between Alaska and Russia. If the last part of this itinerary turned out to be blocked by ice, he might have dodged into Wellington Channel and so back to the comparative safety of Lancaster Sound.

As a glance at a map will show, this suggests a very simplified view of the geographical complexities. But it also gives a pretty clear indication that, if he succeeded, and if he was not compelled to use the bolt hole of Wellington Channel, he would indeed have charted a North-West Passage. Whatever may have been at fault with the expedition (and, so far, there was nothing to show that anything had been), Franklin and Barrow had been working on the right lines when they planned the assault upon this enigmatic part of the Arctic.

Barrow must have been very convincing. He succeeded where others had failed and shook the Admiralty out of its lethargy. In November 1847 the First Lord announced that relief expeditions would be dispatched and that, exceeding Barrow's demands, there would be three of them. The third would be led by Dr (later Sir) John Richardson. Travelling overland, it would follow the course of the Mackenzie River until it debouched into the Beaufort Sea. Lady Franklin, ever anxious to have a say in the matter, promptly contributed £2,000. Her only condition was that the searchers should make a diversion into Prince Regent Inlet. It was in this area, her instinct told her, that her husband might have wintered. (To save you the trouble of looking it up, Lancaster Sound ends in a kind of cross-roads. Turn right, and you are in the Wellington Channel. Proceed straight on and you find yourself in the Barrow Strait. Take the lefthand turn, and you are on a southerly course, passing down Prince Regent Inlet towards the Gulf of Boothia.)

Two ships, *Herald* and *Plover*, under the command of Captain Henry Kellett, took up station in the Bering Strait and then ventured into coastal waters. They found no traces whatsoever of the missing ships. Sir John Richardson encountered

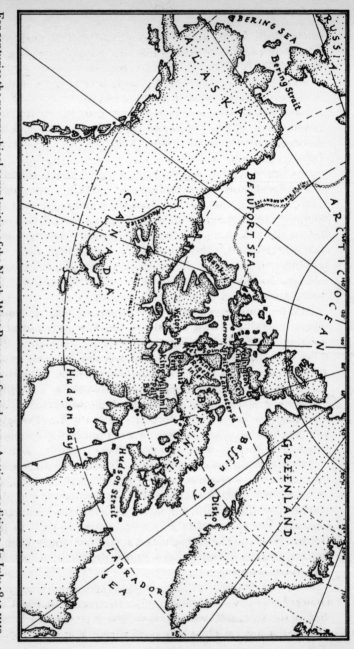

For centuries the geographical complexities of the North-West Passage defeated many Arctic expeditions. In July 1845 HMS *Erebus* and HMS *Terror* were last seen entering the frozen wilderness of Lancaster Sound.

unreasonably bad weather – even for this part of the world – and
made little progress. At some time during the following year, he
returned home, leaving his colleague, Dr John Rae of the
Hudson's Bay Company, to slog on as best he could. Over in
the east, James Ross was no more successful.

His two ships, HMS *Enterprise* and HMS *Investigator*, were
recently built sloops – *Enterprise* under Ross's command and
Investigator with Captain Robert McClure in charge. Ross's
First Lieutenant in *Enterprise* was an unusually intelligent
young officer named Francis McClintock. Later McClintock
was to break some record or other by covering 1,250 miles in
105 days by sledge. The achievement was partly due to his
instinctive understanding of the Eskimos – even to the extent of
asking himself what one of these habitués of the frozen
wilderness would do under a given set of circumstances.

The small vessels – each of about 300 tons – found the middle
of Baffin Bay blocked by a large mass of ice. Nevertheless, they
found a way round it and presently entered Lancaster Sound.
As they probed westwards, they fired their guns at regular
intervals and, at night, sent up rockets. Any Eskimo in the
vicinity may have wondered what all the fuss was about: but,
from the Franklin expedition, there was no answer. Ross also
dropped small casks overboard at daily intervals. Inside each
were documents explaining his tactics. Hopefully one or two
might reach *Erebus* and *Terror* and at least provide assurance
that help was on the way. In fact, it was about as useless as
addressing a letter to someone in France, placing it inside a
bottle, and dropping it into the sea at Dover.

When at last *Enterprise* and *Investigator* reached the meeting of
the ways at the western end of Lancaster Sound, the ingenious
Ross devised another measure. He sent his men out to hunt
Arctic foxes. They might employ whatever methods they liked
– so long as they brought the animals back alive. Once he had
accumulated what he judged to be a sufficient number, he fitted
collars fashioned from copper to their necks. Each was
engraved with the positions of his ships and the supply dumps
that he had established. Then the creatures were released. It
may seem to have been a somewhat haphazard undertaking;
but, in this situation, what else was there to do?

In the spring (of 1849) he sent off parties of men on sledges, each of them covering about fifty miles. The Eskimos they encountered obviously wished to be helpful, but they could tell them nothing. In the end, Ross had to give up. The mystery of John Franklin, the *Erebus*, the *Terror*, and the 139 officers and ratings was no closer to a solution. Indeed, as those of a realistic turn of mind argued, the matter was now becoming largely one of academic interest. After such a long time, there could be little hope of finding any survivors. The Arctic had done its best to close the file on the North-West Passage.

Back in England, however, a 'Find Franklin' campaign was in full cry – much of it generated by the explorer's wife. Shop windows featured Arctic displays. In the pleasure gardens at Vauxhall in London the big attraction for 1849 was a diorama of Arctic scenery. The Government offered £20,000 to anyone who rescued the missing men; £10,000 for the rescue of one of them, or for information that led to such a feat; and, in the event of no such happy outcome, £10,000 for a solution to the mystery.

Lady Franklin still had hope – or appeared to. She wrote regular letters to her husband and was undaunted when they were returned to her. At her suggestion, a day of public prayer was held to plead for the safety of all those who were serving in Arctic regions. And, as so frequently happens, the hoaxers with their perverted senses of humour, made the most of the opportunity. Bottles were washed up on the coast with faked messages inside them. Rumours were circulated. According to one, a message from Franklin had been found on a balloon that landed in Gloucestershire. There was a story that Eskimos had heard guns fired from the *Erebus* and *Terror*, and a fictitious account of the two ships being washed up on the coast of Newfoundland.

Having committed itself to the offer of rewards, there was no going back for the Admiralty. In the autumn of 1850 a fleet of fifteen ships set out from various places – among them two brigs that had formerly been the property of the United States Navy and had been acquired by a retired shipping magnate named Henry Grinnell. Mr Grinnell, it seems, had been greatly moved by Lady Franklin's pleas for help and wanted to do his bit.

Again, the plan was for a pincer movement, although on a rather larger scale than that of 1848–9. A small fleet under the command of Captain Austin advanced from Lancaster Sound.

Among the ships were the barques *Resolute* and *Assistance*, the screw-propelled steamers *Pioneer* and *Intrepid* (the first proper steam ships to navigate through ice), two brigs – the *Sophia* and the *Lady Franklin* (commanded by whaling ship masters), a schooner named *Felix* and a supply ship (both contributions from the Hudson's Bay Company), Mr Grinnell's two brigs, and another sailing ship (the *Prince Albert*) that had been fitted out by Lady Franklin and a number of her friends (which may account for her contribution of £2,000). On land, Dr John Rae resumed his efforts that were little short of heroic. And, over in the west, a smaller force consisting of McClure in *Investigator*, *Enterprise* (Captain Collinson), and *Plover* (Captain Kellett), made its way to the Bering Sea by way of the Magellan Straits.

The idea was that *Plover* should remain in the Bering Strait, acting, so to speak, as long stop. *Investigator* and *Enterprise* would work their respective ways eastwards – possibly meeting up eventually with Captain Austin's ships. The flaw in its execution was that Captain McClure appears to have been more concerned to discover the missing North-West Passage than he was to find clues about what might have befallen *Erebus* and *Terror*. He pushed on regardless of anything that Captain Collinson might be doing, and his efforts were rewarded. He did, indeed, find the key to this particular mystery, but no traces of the missing Franklin expedition. It was magnificent, but it was not in the nature of this particular enterprise. The two ships should have been working as a team: one covering the northern coastline – the other, the southern. To make matters even more difficult, the only interpreter of the Eskimo tongue happened to be in *Investigator*. Collinson met several parties of Eskimos who clearly had something to say and who wanted to say it. But there was no means of comprehending what it was.

What was more, McClure overreached himself. His ship became trapped in the ice as winter closed in and all but two members of the crew succumbed to scurvy. Collinson, too, seemed to be in trouble or, at least, overdue. Consequently two more vessels were now added to the score of missing ships.

Over in the east, however, Captain Austin's group had done better. The credit belongs to the brigs contributed by Henry Grinnell. They came at last to Beechey Island, a small slab of land not far from the entrance to the Barrow Strait (or, if you prefer it, at the Lancaster Sound crossroads). Here they found indisputable evidence that *Erebus* and *Terror* had passed the first winter in the area. There was a storehouse: a forge, a shooting gallery, many cans of food and a greater amount of litter. There were also marks to suggest that a sledge, carrying a heavy load, had been hauled over the snow – and three small tombstones marking the graves of a stoker from HMS *Terror*, a seaman and a marine from HMS *Erebus*. It filled in a scrap of the story, but not sufficient. Ironically, other ships had come within a few miles of more fruitful clues without realizing it. The mystery remained unsolved.

In 1852 another attempt was made. The commander on this occasion was 53-year-old Captain Edward Belcher. He took with him five ships – *Resolute*, *North Star*, *Assistance*, *Intrepid* and *Pioneer*. It was a formidable assignment, for Belcher was not merely looking for information about Franklin: he also had *Investigator* and *Enterprise* on his list of missing ships. *Enterprise*, as it happened, was not in need of assistance, but *Investigator* certainly was. By one of those happy chances that occasionally favour members of the human race, a lieutenant from HMS *Resolute*, travelling by sledge overland, came upon the stranded ship just as McClure was about to abandon her. An hour or so later, the crew of the *Investigator* would have suffered a fate similar to that of Franklin's men. As it was, they returned safely to England, where the House of Commons granted McClure a knighthood and £5,000 – plus another £5,000 to be shared out among the ship's company. It was their reward for being (or seeming to be) the discoverers of the North-West Passage.

It was during Belcher's expedition that McClintock made his epic journey by sledge, but in terms of Franklin the achievement had to be considered negative. Nor did Belcher return in triumph. For some unaccountable reason, he decided to leave all his ships except the *North Star* behind. With everybody crammed on board her, she must have been horribly overcrowded. The fact that it was unnecessary was shown beyond all reasonable doubt some while later, when *Resolute* was discovered by the crew of a whaler working in the Davis Strait. She was in perfectly good order. After a refit in a New England dockyard, she was returned to the British Admiralty and thus back into service. Belcher was court martialled for his strange conduct. He was acquitted: eventually promoted to Admiral and given the customary knighthood.

Meanwhile, the industrious Dr Rae, working on land, had discovered more Franklin evidence. At a place named Pelly Bay, he came across an Eskimo who had a strange tale to relate. Four years previously, it seems, a party of white men had been observed struggling over the frozen sea off Prince William Island. Their ships, apparently, had been crushed by ice: they had run out of food and they were now proposing to hunt game on the mainland. Some while later, other Eskimos discovered the bodies of thirty-five men as well as a gun and some ammunition. According to Dr Rae's informant, everything indicated that they had failed to find any wildlife and had taken to cannibalism. It was a horrible story and the doctor's initial reaction was to disbelieve it. But the Eskimo produced several objects to substantiate part of it. Among them was a small silver plate inscribed with the name of Sir John Franklin.

Dr Rae hurried back to his base at York Factory on Hudson's Bay to report the matter. The news eventually reached Barrow's successor at the Admiralty in London. But, by this time, the Royal Navy had more pressing concerns than the fate of an expedition that had been missing for nine years. The Crimean War had broken out.

It was now 1854. Officially, it was at last assumed that Franklin and his men had 'died on Her Majesty's Service'. Lady Franklin, however, was not prepared to accept the assumption. She refused a widow's pension, put on her brightest clothes and redoubled her efforts. Perhaps she was encouraged by a ballad that was on sale in the streets of London. The title was: 'Lady Franklin's Lament'. It went like this:

> My Franklin dear long has been gone
> To explore the northern seas,
> I wonder if my faithful John,
> Is still battling with the breeze;
> Or if e'er he will return again,
> To these fond arms once more
> To heal the wounds of dearest Jane,
> Whose heart is grieved full sore.

Well then . . . pretty horrible, really. But at least it showed sympathy and sympathy was something Lady Franklin badly needed when the information about Dr Rae's discovery reached her. She could no longer expect any help from the Admiralty, but this did not deter this remarkable woman. She decided to go it alone.

In the early 1850s, a steam yacht named the *Fox* had been built in Aberdeen for Sir Richard Sutton Bt – a sportsman who, according to the *Concise Dictionary of National Biography*, was 'one of the most wealthy men in the country' (for some years, he bore the entire cost of running the Quorn hunt in Leicestershire). In 1855 Sir Richard took his ship to Norway in search of salmon fishing. Shortly after his return to Britain, he died and his executors put the 300-ton screw steamer onto the market. Lady Franklin, assisted by friends who never seemed to run out of money or generosity, bought her for the sum of £2,000. Francis McClintock (now promoted to captain) was invited to command her. The vessel was stripped of all her fineries and fitted out to accommodate a crew of twenty-six for a period of twenty-eight months. As McClintock was to write:

The velvet hangings and splendid furniture of the yacht, and also everything not contributing part of the vessel's strengthening were to be removed; the large skylights and capacious ladderways had to be reduced to limits more adapted to a polar clime; the whole vessel to be externally sheathed with stout planking, and internally fortified by strong cross beams, longitudinal beams, iron staunchions and diagonal fastenings; the false keel taken off, the slender brass propeller replaced by a massive iron one, the boiler taken out, altered and enlarged; the sharp stem to be cased in iron until it resembled a ponderous chisel set up edgeways; even the yacht's rig had to be altered. (*The Fate of Sir John Franklin*, 1859).

Some idea of the accommodation is suggested by the dimensions of the wardroom that had to house five officers. It measured eight feet square. Nevertheless, despite the cramped conditions, the *Fox* was an harmonious ship. As McClintock wrote, there was an atmosphere of '. . . mutual esteem and goodwill, which made our ship's company a happy little community, and contributed materially to the success of the expedition'.

For the expedition *was* a success: it succeeded where much bigger ventures had failed. It filled in the final evidence of what had happened to *Erebus* and *Terror* and all who sailed in them.

On 1 July 1857 the *Fox* sailed from Aberdeen. She spent her first Arctic winter in Baffin Bay; her second in Bellot Strait, a narrow channel joining Peel Sound with Prince Regent Inlet. From here, McClintock and one of his officers, Lieutenant Hobson, travelled across the Boothia Peninsula and then over the ice to King William Island. On the west coast of the island at a place now known as Point Victory, Hobson came across a cairn. Beside it, there was a metal box containing a log of the last days of *Erebus* and *Terror*. It recorded that Franklin had died aboard his ship in June of 1847. The two vessels had been wedged in the ice for nineteen months: by 25 April 1848 another twenty-four had died. The last entry stated that 105 men, commanded by Captain Crozier, were about to set off in a final, desperate, search for food.

Some distance away, McClintock was told by Eskimos that a ship had been wrecked on the western shore of the island. An old woman recalled that men had marched away to the south and that, one by one, they had died. McClintock followed up these clues and, sure enough, he found a skeleton wearing the uniform of a steward in the Royal Navy. A pocket comb and a clothes brush lay on the ground beside him. Later, he discovered a small boat mounted on a sledge with two more skeletons in it. There were some books (including a copy of *The Vicar of Wakefield*), a supply of tea, some tobacco, and twenty-six items of plate.

As a glance at a map suggests, this was sufficient to show that Franklin's men had discovered the key to the North-West Passage – though, in their enfeebled state, they probably did not realize it. The *Fox* returned to England in 1859, calling at Portsmouth on 21 September to set McClintock ashore. Parliament rewarded him and his crew with £5,000. The Royal Geographical Society recognized that the Franklin expedition had, in fact, found the elusive Passage before McClure, and presented Lady Franklin with its Founder's Medal. During the next twenty years, more details of the tragic if triumphant expedition were filled in by two members of the United States Army – Captain Charles Francis Hall and Lieutenant

Schwatka. The route of Crozier's final march was marked by skeletons, graves and relics. The Eskimos had many things to tell them – including the location of one of the ships. The first time they saw it, the locals had managed to board it. Somewhat to their consternation, they saw the body of a white man sprawled out on the deck. At some later date, the vessel foundered and only the tops of the masts could be seen above the ice.

From such evidence, it was possible to reconstruct what had happened. It was fair to assume that, having negotiated Lancaster Sound, Franklin found his proposed route blocked by ice in Barrow Strait. He therefore turned north along the Wellington Channel – where, again, he was probably thwarted by ice. For want of any alternative, he spent the first winter (1845–6) off Beechey Island at the Lancaster Sound crossroads.

In the spring, he headed southwards down Peel Sound until, probably on 12 September, the ships were again trapped by ice – this time off Victory Point. This, it can be assumed, was their final resting place. A Lieutenant Gore went ashore with a party, built the cairn and left the box containing his log beneath it. When he returned to *Erebus*, he found that Franklin had died: many of the men were ill and there was a disastrous shortage of food. Captain Crozier decided that the only hope of survival lay on shore. The ships were abandoned and the tragic march began.

This is a fair solution to the mystery, but it poses other questions. So many ships were involved in the search for Franklin and his men, and yet only McClure and his *Investigator* came to any harm – and he and most of his crew were rescued. Why, then, were *Erebus* and *Terror* singled out for such tragic endings? Did Franklin blunder? No. The matter can only be explained by appalling luck. But the strangest thing of all is that the Franklin expedition did not perish in an unpopulated region. The Eskimos came and went and flourished. Somewhere in this frozen wilderness, there was the means of supporting life, but the crews of *Erebus* and *Terror* were unable to find it. Dying, they were actually seen by these people who possessed a secret more precious than that of the North-West Passage.

McClure, McClintock, Kellett and Collinson, even the ship-abandoning Belcher – they all prospered in the service and became Admirals. Lady Franklin died in 1875 at the age of seventy-three, but not before she had seen a memorial to her husband erected in Westminster Abbey. As for the North-West Passage, it finally fell to the Norwegian explorer Roald Amundsen who began his journey along it in 1903 with a small crew and a fishing sloop as his transport. Admittedly, it took him three years, but he accomplished it. Very much more recently, it has been negotiated by the nuclear submarine USS *Nautilus* and, in 1969, by the Humble Oil Company's tanker *Manhattan* laden with a cargo of Alaskan crude oil. She received substantial damage, which begs the question: was it ever worth seeking in the first place? As a commercial proposition it was never viable. On the other hand, the search for it put many Arctic regions on the map, and there are names to prove it: McClure Strait, McClintock Channel, Amundsen Gulf, and Franklin Island. And, indeed, how much poorer the human race would be if there had not been men who wanted to see what lay around the next corner.

8

Crack Up

Sometime during the night of 9 September 1980, the 91,654 tons gross (169,044 deadweight) combination carrier *Derbyshire* disappeared. She was nearly twice as big as the *Titanic*; her massive length of 300 yards was roughly that of three football pitches. Nevertheless, a typhoon with the oddly inappropriate name of 'Orchid' erased her from the ocean. It also accounted for Captain Geoffrey Underhill, the ship's master, his crew of forty-one officers and ratings, and the wives of two officers. The only traces of *Derbyshire*'s existence were one lifeboat (empty) and some slicks of oil upon the unquiet ocean. But the oil was inconclusive. It might have come from some other ship.

Between the 7th and the 15th of the previous April, the *Derbyshire* had been drydocked at Sasebo in Japan. This was an annual examination for classification purposes carried out by Lloyd's Register of Shipping. At the same time, her lifeboat falls were renewed, a fracture in the welds on a transverse bulkhead was repaired, and damage to her starboard bilge keel was put right. None of this was serious: *Derbyshire* had passed what a landsman might call her MoT test. On 18 April she sailed for Hay Point in Australia, loaded a cargo of coal, and on 1 May departed for Fos-sur-Mer, near Marseille. During the voyage, she ran into bad weather and sustained minor injuries, but they were nothing that her crew could not remedy. At Fos-sur-Mer, her then master, Captain Peter Boyle, went off on leave. He was replaced by Captain Underhill.

On 23 June *Derbyshire* set off for New York. Among those present on board was a representative of Marine Safety

Services Ltd, a firm of consultants employed by *Derbyshire*'s owners, Bibby Tankers Ltd. During the voyage, he carried out a safety training programme and inspected the ship's lifesaving equipment. Such defects as he found were put right. At New York the vessel took on fuel, and on 7 July set course for Sept-Iles (otherwise known as Seven Islands) in the Saint Lawrence where she arrived three days later. One hundred and fifty-seven thousand tons of iron ore were loaded into her holds. Within less than a week she was on passage to Kawasaki in Japan. The trip, which was routed by way of the Cape of Good Hope, should have taken about two months. There was no reason to believe that she would fail to make it. Experts had judged her condition to be satisfactory; her crew, most of them from Liverpool, had been properly tutored in the procedures for safety at sea.

Somewhere off the tip of Southern Africa, a helicopter replenished her supplies on 8 August and took off mail from members of her crew. Among the correspondence was a letter to his mother from one of the engineers. He didn't appear to have absolute confidence in his ship. He described her as 'a big lumbering thing'. As he explained, she 'doesn't ride over the waves as any normal ship would, but just ploughs straight through everything. For the last week, with quite a heavy sea running, we've hardly seen the foredeck. She also bends in the middle quite a lot, so looks a bit like a caterpillar going along. Don't get alarmed about the bending in the middle bit, she's designed to. After all, being nearly a thousand feet long, she'd break in half in bad weather if she didn't bend – just like a fresh carrot.'

The voyage dragged on. By 3 September she was to the south of Mindanao in the Philippines, heading for what the discerning reader will recognize as 'The Devil's Sea'. On this day, Captain Underhill received his first warning of trouble to come. It was a weather map facsimile transmitted from Japan and indicating a possible tropical depression more than 1,000 miles away to the east.

Among a ship's guardians in the everlasting war against the weather is a California-based firm called Ocean Routes. Bibby's subscribed to its services. Captain Underhill informed it about the depression and said that he had increased

Derbyshire's speed from 10 to 12.5 knots. Next day, Ocean Routes advised him that he should give the depression a miss by at least 200 nautical miles, and recommended a course and a speed that should have achieved this. However, you can foresee with reasonable accuracy where a ship will be at a particular moment; you cannot, on the other hand, foretell what a meteorological eruption will do. In circumstances such as these, it is as well to prevent (or try to) the one converging upon the other – though that may be difficult.

Noon on the 6th found the ship and the depression separated by 880 miles. The former was her usual substantial self, the latter was increasing in its nastiness. Later in the day, its status was upgraded to that of a tropical revolving storm (or typhoon) and the name 'Orchid' was used for the first time. It was following a complex, curving route and travelling at about the same speed as *Derbyshire*. Captain Underhill, with assistance from Ocean Routes, was doing all the right things, but 'Orchid' was a wiley opponent. Quite often it cheated and its size and fury were growing. By the 9th, winds of 80 knots were expected in places – though where they would be nobody could tell with any certainty.

Derbyshire was not quite alone. On the 9th, a motor vessel named the *Alrai* was less than 100 miles away from her and the two ships had obviously been talking to each other. On that day, the *Alrai*'s chief officer sent the following report: 'R/O (radio operator) of *Alrai* received noon position and speed of *Derbyshire* 80 miles distant from *Alrai*. It was calculated that *Derbyshire* would be approx. 60 miles from *Alrai* at 23.00/9th. Storm was deepest on *Alrai* at that time. Barometer 962, wave heights 60–100ft. Wind force 12. Vis. nil. Chief officer last feels that it should not be ruled out that the *Derbyshire* broke down and broached to.'

As this may suggest, 'Orchid' had already won. On 6 September, Captain Underhill had radioed his estimated time of arrival at Kawasaki as noon on the 11th. Forty-eight hours later, he amended it. It seemed that he was stormbound and likely to be one day late. On the 9th he had spoken again – and, so far as the outside world was concerned, for the last time. His ship was now hove-to 700 nautical miles to the south-south-west of Tokyo Bay. His ETA was amended to sometime on the

14th – to which he added the word 'hopefully'. Captain Underhill's hopes were not to be fulfilled. The *Derbyshire* was never seen nor heard from again. There was no notice of her going, no May Day signal, nothing. Whatever had happened must have occurred very suddenly, giving the forty-four people on board no chance to call for help; not even, one assumes, the opportunity to abandon ship.

Returning to the chief officer of the *Alrai*'s report, *had* the *Derbyshire*'s engine broken down, or had there been some other mechanical failure? If there had not been, why did Captain Underhill stop his ship? In such circumstances, a degree of agility was essential – not least to avoid the situation of becoming beam-on to those massive seas that were running. The waves would have crashed across her main deck – exploding on her hatch covers, pounding, perhaps, on her stern. The trouble would have been very considerable: a mariner of Captain Underhill's experience would never have willingly allowed his ship to become so vulnerable.

A landsman may, perhaps, be forgiven if he finds the reactions to the *Derbyshire*'s vanishing act curiously lethargic. The ship disappeared on the 9th. To put it another way, no word was heard from her after that day. But it was not until the 13th that Bibby's instructed their agents in Japan to ask the Japanese Maritime Safety Agency to mount a search. The Japanese Maritime Safety Agency shook its collective head and said that no such operation could take place until the vessel was at least 24 hours overdue. Captain Underhill had given his probable date of arrival as the 14th. Personnel at a number of radio stations were asked to keep their ears open for any information about the vessel, but it was not until the 15th that the patrol ships *Osumi* and *Motobu*, assisted by two reconnaissance aircraft, were dispatched in search of the missing vessel. On that and on the following day, the oil slicks were sighted.

But the weather had not yet finished with the *Derbyshire* case. On the 17th another storm – codenamed 'Sperry' – unleashed its fury and the operation had to be interrupted for 24 hours. Finally after no more traces were found, it was abandoned during the late afternoon of the 20th. More than a month later, the empty lifeboat was discovered by the Japanese tanker *Daiei Maru*. It had nothing to offer in the way of clues to the

Derbyshire's fate, and the tanker's captain did not bother to recover it.

In England, a memorial service for the ship's complement was held in Liverpool Cathedral, relief funds were set up for crew's dependents, and the Department of Transport initiated a preliminary inquiry. Several months later, Lord Trefgarne, then Parliamentary Under Secretary of State for Trade, announced that, owing to lack of any evidence, a formal investigation would serve no useful purpose. On the other hand, he promised to reconsider his decision 'should any new and material evidence come to light.' No such evidence ever did come to light and now, as then, the *Derbyshire*'s fate can only be a matter of conjecture. As Mr J. Kinahan, Special Services Officer of the National Union of Seamen, pointed out in a BBC interview, the prospects of discovering the truth would have been very much better had she been an aircraft. Aeroplanes are fitted with flight recorders that can be recovered – even from the ocean. Provided the lines of communication have not been ruptured the tapes reveal virtually everything that has happened during the minutes and seconds before the disaster. Ships are not so equipped. A voyage recorder, costing about £400,000 is available. A radio beacon enables it to be located – even if a vessel equipped with it has foundered in deep water. Nor need its use be confined to emergencies. It can supply the master and his crew with information; it can also record knowledge that might lead to improvements in design.

But shipowners have not responded to the idea. In the midst of a world slump, their concern seems to be concentrated on running their fleets at the minimum cost. As I remarked in an earlier chapter, during recent years the improvements made in the cause of safety at sea do not seem to have matched those applied to the airline business. This particularly concerns the investigation of accidents. In Britain at any rate, these are not judicial inquiries. The Department of Transport's responsibility is simply to discover what went wrong. Given the cause, it may be able to prevent a recurrence of the effect. But there is an urgency about seeking the reasons for aircraft crashes that does not seem to follow in the wake of merchant ship disasters. The difference, of course, is that the freight of airliners is people. Ships, nowadays, are mostly carriers of commodities – and, even in the hey-day of the big liners, the record was not altogether impressive (read any book you like about the *Titanic*). It is, perhaps, symptomatic of an industry that, like shipbuilding itself, rarely enjoys economic stability.

Mr Kinahan also drew attention to the reluctance of governments to conduct formal investigations into maritime disasters. During the past five years, he explained, there had been 111 'very serious' cases. Only four of them had been the subjects of such inquiries.

Eventually, on 11 June 1987, the Secretary of State for Transport directed that a Formal Investigation into the *Derbyshire*'s loss should be held. No 'new and material evidence' had come to light – unless one considers the loss, towards the end of 1986, of one of *Derbyshire*'s sisters. This brought to a head eight years of conjecture and dissatisfaction – years in which serious doubts had been cast on the integrity of the vessels' construction. The time had come, so to speak, to see whether anything had been swept under the carpet. And so it was that, on 5 October 1987, the Wreck Commissioner (Mr G. R. A. Darling, RD, QC) and three Assessors convened at Church House, Westminster. This part of the investigation lasted 46 days. Afterwards, on 23 March 1988, they went to Rotterdam where they inspected the *Sir Alexander Glen* – another of *Derbyshire*'s sisters. The Court's findings were published on 18 January 1989 – *more than eight years after the disaster*. The verdict was predictable: the *Derbyshire* 'was probably overwhelmed by the forces of nature, but whether that is what actually happened must remain a matter of speculation.' This is a repetition, almost word for word, of the conclusion reached in March 1986, when the Department of Transport published the second of two reports on the loss of the ship. On this occasion, the statement was: 'In the last analysis, the cause of the loss of *Derbyshire* is, and will almost certainly remain, a matter of speculation.' All of which is quite correct, although this version overlooks a paragraph included in the earlier report. It read:

If *Derbyshire* was constructed in much the same way as the sister ships, and there is little reason to suppose that she was not, then in the severe tropical storm which occurred, major cracking possibly developed as it did in *Tyne Bridge* (q.v.) In the case of *Derbyshire*, it is most likely that, had cracking taken place, it is probable that it took place so rapidly and extensively that total structural failure resulted. This was followed by the capsizal of the inhabited portion of the ship abaft frame 65. This probably accounts for the complete absence of any distress traffic.

Frame 65! It attracted a lot of attention – not only in that initial Department of Transport report, but also in the deliberations of two organizations (the British Ship Research Association and a firm of consultants named Bishop, Price and Partners) employed by the Department's Marine Directorate to consider the ship's construction. At times, it appeared to be the key to the whole mystery, but the Formal Inquiry more or less absolved it of blame. Under 'Summary of Conclusions', the report says: 'The combination of circumstances necessary to postulate separation of the hull at frame No. 65 is very unlikely . . .' However, hedging its bets, it adds: '. . . though some element of doubt must remain.' The remains of the *Derbyshire* will never be discovered. Without them, it can neither be blamed nor given complete absolution.

Perhaps, then, we should forget about Frame 65.

It is, however, less easy to erase from the mind the remarks of Professor Richard Bishop – The Bishop of Bishop, Price and Partners and also vice-chancellor of Brunel University in Middlesex. In a television programme he said, 'She, the *Derbyshire*, was a large ship, cavernous inside. There was not the honeycomb of a liner or a warship. And there would be nothing to stop a crack propagating round the hull.' In a similar programme on Radio 4, he said, 'There is a much bigger issue than the *Derbyshire* – massive though she is. If ships are going to get bigger and bigger, longer and longer, heavier and heavier, a complete change in the techniques of naval architectural structural analysis will have to take place. We are concerned with bulk carriers and with tankers, and the point there is that these ships are like cathedrals. If a crack starts in the main hull, there's nothing to arrest it . . . If they don't start rethinking ship design, then I'm afraid we're going to have another sequence of failure when the ships are long and heavy.' Yes, he agreed, there could be another *Derbyshire* case.

There was, of course, no want of theories about what *might* have happened during those dreadful moments when 'Orchid' was raging – of how such a large and seemingly well-ordered ship could have been such an easy prey for the monstrous storm. Among them were the following:

Explosion. But the *Derbyshire* had not carried crude oil since October 1979 – nearly a year earlier. The holds had been satisfactorily cleaned out afterwards and certified as free from any risk of explosions caused by gas. The hypothesis cannot survive serious examination.

Water getting into her holds and making the iron ore yet heavier. This could certainly have caused her to founder, but not suddenly. It would have been a slowish process, allowing ample time in which to transmit a distress signal and, indeed, to abandon ship. The behaviour of the vessel would have become sluggish; she'd have settled deeper into the water. A master with Captain Underhill's expertise would certainly have been forewarned in plenty of time to take appropriate action.

But did he try to send a May Day signal? Were his cries for assistance unheard because the radio antennae had been destroyed by the storm? In this case, the destruction of the *Derbyshire* might not have been so sudden and cataclysmic. But no, this appeared unlikely. The components were made by a German firm with a very high reputation in this field of industry. It might have been a convenient explanation, but it was not convincing. In any case, it only ventured a solution to one small aspect of the problem. The *Derbyshire* foundered. Damaged, or destroyed, radio antennae do not cause ships to sink.

Engine failure was an obvious possibility. It would have accounted for Captain Underhill's apparent inability to control the ship in its battle against the waves. But it need not have explained the lack of distress signals. The radio had a back-up system and the *Alrai* was not all that far away.

Finally, there was this question of whether there was some inherent weakness in her construction: a factor that the stresses of typhoon 'Orchid' pushed beyond its limits – causing the carrier to break up. Of all the options, this seemed to be the most plausible, and it was this that received the most attention.

The origins of the *Derbyshire* go back to the late 1960s, when Swan Hunter conceived a plan to build this type of combination carrier. Between 1971 and 1976, six of them were completed at the Haverton Hill shipyard. The first of the sextet of giants, the *Furness Bridge*, was launched by the Duchess of Kent and cost £20 million. On her sea trials, Mr Hartley Reed, the owners' superintendent, suggested that it might be as well to make sure her cargo tanks were in good order. After all, Swan Hunter had never built anything like this before. The shipbuilders' management seemed to be reluctant. In the end, however, they agreed to test one of them. Water was pumped in and the result was alarming. Far from withstanding the input, it became seriously fractured in several places. In the light of this disturbing evidence, the other tanks were given the same treatment. Six of the nine developed severe fractures – due to defective welding.

But this was not the end of the matter. Later, the *Furness Bridge* developed more cracks and had to be dry-docked at Genoa. Among her visitors was Mr Reed. He described the damage as 'extremely serious and frightening'. As he pointed out, the fault was well on the way towards running all the way round the vessel. 'The ship would have broken in two had we not discovered it,' he said.

Swan Hunter, it should be stressed, has a substantial reputation for building fine ships. Nor, at any time, has there been criticism of the designs that were approved by Lloyd's Register of Shipping. However, not far from the Haverton Hill yard, another firm was building rigs for the North Sea oil industry. The rates of pay were better than those at Swan Hunter. Not surprisingly, then, the best of the shipyard's welders took their services to the place where the rewards were greater. This left a gap in the work force at a time when, unlike the sorry conditions that are a feature of Teesside nowadays, skilled labour was not all that easy to find.

Replacements were hired, but is there reason to suppose that their abilities may have been inferior to those of the men who had gone elsewhere? The answer must be 'no'. Before joining the firm's payroll, the newcomers' skills were tested, and afterwards they underwent a period of training. According to the Formal Inquiry's report, 'Examples were quoted by witnesses, concerning the construction of the earlier ships of the Class, of sub-standard welding ... It was claimed that all faults when observed were corrected. There was no evidence to show that these or any other welding faults persisted during the building of the later ships and particularly the *Derbyshire* or that any faults which were detected were more numerous than would have been found in any other high class UK shipyard at that time.'

One by one, the giant carriers came into service. The *Furness Bridge* was followed by the *Tyne Bridge*; then came the *English Bridge*, *Sir John Hunter* (later *Cast Kittiwake*), *Alexander Glen* and finally, the *Derbyshire*. In several cases, their names have since been changed and they have passed into foreign ownership. Two are now operating under the Italian flag, one is owned by a company in Taiwan, and a fourth belongs to a Japanese company though with Liberian registration. None of them has been without problems.

Immediately after the *Derbyshire* vanished, the Bibby line convened a meeting at which representatives of all the other owners were present. Each was asked whether he had experienced any difficulties with his vessel, and each replied in the negative. Strangely, the matter of the *Furness Bridge*'s cargo tanks during her sea trials does not seem to have been mentioned. It was, after all, the first clue that all was not entirely well. However, this was only 1980. Whatever jinx it was that bedevilled the sorry six had not yet had sufficient time in which to work all its evil mischief.

Ironically, it had begun its catalogue of misfortunes in the *Derbyshire* – the last of the sextet. Before setting out on her maiden voyage in 1976, she was lying alongside a quay at Antwerp. The auxiliary boiler's furnace suddenly ruptured. The third engineer was killed by the released pressure. Later the ship's electrician died of injuries. Then, four years afterwards, the very ship herself vanished, removing all traces of the forty-four people on board. But this was by no means the end. It had other, less spectacular, devilments in store.

For example, the *Tyne Bridge* was outward bound from Hamburg in 1982 when she ran into heavy weather in the

North Sea. The captain was alarmed by the sound of cracking coming from the area of the deck immediately in front of the bridge. Afraid that the ship was about to break in two, he issued a May Day signal. Three German search and rescue helicopters responded. Twenty-eight members of the crew were evacuated. The helicopters then stood by as, with the remainder of her complement still on board, the apparently stricken vessel managed to limp back to Hamburg. She was put into dry dock and the hull examined. There certainly were cracks, although not so serious as the master had imagined. Nevertheless, extensive repairs were needed, and the ship remained in dry dock for the next three weeks.

Not long afterwards, the *Cast Kittiwake* found herself in similar trouble, though no rescue operation had to be mounted. Cracks had developed in frame 65 – at roughly the same place in which they had occurred in the *Tyne Bridge*. She put into Rotterdam, where the defect was diagnosed and put right. Was this, then, a failing common to all of them? The fifth ship in the series, the *Sir Alexander Glen*, was at sea carrying a cargo of iron ore at the time. Her master was called up on the radio and asked to look for anything out of the ordinary – especially in the areas of No. 65 bulkhead. He found that there were cracks and that, indeed, they had developed in the same location as that of the *Tyne Bridge*'s flaws. When the vessel reached her destination in Southern Italy, the damaged area was re-welded.

But this was not the end of the matter. Seven weeks later, the cracks reappeared – in more or less the same place. Welding, then, was obviously not the answer. Some more drastic cure was required: upon this point Lloyd's and the other classification societies that were now involved agreed.

To put matters right, owners were recommended to cut out sections of the frame: to fit a new length of girder that passed through it, and to replace the deck plates in the area with a stronger grade of steel.

Reading through the mass of documents relating to the loss of the *Derbyshire*, the number of opinions voiced on radio and television, one has the impression of two sides locked in combat. On the one hand, we find the views of the dead men's relatives and of experts who – either for personal reasons (for example, Mr Peter Ridyard, a marine surveyor whose son had been one of the victims), or because they were employed to do so – tried to investigate the disaster. In some instances, they produced surprising revelations. Professor Bishop, for example, was asked in the television programme whether, in the light of mishaps that occurred to the other vessels in this sad sextet, he was not 'being clever by hindsight'. Said Professor Bishop, 'To tell the truth, we didn't know she had any sister ships, and we certainly did not know about the cracking that occurred in them.' Surely this suggests a curious omission? The Department of Trade's explanation was: 'If those conducting the research had been apprised of the defects, it was thought that the motivation to pursue the lines of inquiry that they had been set might have been lost.' It was rather like suggesting that a detective might lose interest in an investigation if he were given an important clue.

On the other side, there were those who wished (or seemed to wish) that the ghost of the *Derbyshire* would go away. Perhaps they were more realistic. To quote Lord Trefgarne again, little could be achieved unless 'new material evidence (came) to light.' None did. The *Derbyshire* had taken her grim secret into the depths of that awful sea.

But the ghost would not go away. By their own misfortunes, the other members of the sad sextet did not allow their sister to rest in peace. In the early winter of 1986, we find the *Kowloon Bridge* (formerly the *English Bridge* and by this time registered in Hong Kong) on passage from Canada to Clydeside with a cargo of ore. At some point, when the ship was struggling against an Atlantic storm, cracks were reported at the after end. Concerned for the safety of his vessel, the master, Captain S. T. Reo, put into Bantry Bay, Ireland. Surveyors from the British and Irish authorities carried out an inspection. The weather was still appalling with winds gusting to 74 mph. Captain Reo was advised to remain where he was.

But the meteorological furies decided otherwise. The *Kowloon Bridge* dragged her anchor and Captain Reo had to proceed seawards whether he liked the idea or not. Ten miles off the coast, the wisdom of the surveyors became all too apparent. The giant carrier lost her rudder and began to ship water. In response to a May Day signal, two Sea King helicopters took off from an RAF base in Wales. Despite considerable difficulties, the 28-man crew was winched to safety. For the *Kowloon Bridge* there was no reprieve. She plunged on to the Stags Rocks in the Fastnet area and broke her back.

On the debit side, then, there was one ship and some 5,000 seabirds that were killed by the seepage of oil. On the credit side, the Department of Transport at last agreed to a Formal Investigation into the loss of the *Derbyshire*. Whatever doubts may have been expressed during the years that separated this investigation from the wreck, its conclusions emphasized that the ship had been 'properly designed, properly built and constructed from material of approved standard.' The cargo and its loading were above suspicion. Captain Underhill's actions were 'not unreasonable'. And so on. Indeed, far from solving the mystery, it tended to increase it. There was no facile way of explaining what had cost those 44 people their lives. 'Orchid' was the killer – there was no doubt about that. But 'Orchid' was unpredictable. Even nowadays, with satellites to observe typhoons, 'the task of forecasting their path, with acceptable accuracy, is, however, complex and remains to this day very difficult.'

Nature, as so often happens, had the last word. The solution to the case of the *Derbyshire* lay not in the ship but in the circumstances. Unless some amazing discovery takes place one day, they will always have the power to baffle.

· This is reflected in the Formal Investigation's recommendations. Mr Darling and his colleagues urged that marine searches should be started more quickly. They argued that mariners' guidance for avoiding tropical revolving storms should be revised: for instance, no attempt should be made to get out of the way by crossing ahead of the storm's probable path (it might put on a burst of speed and reduce the margin of safety). The only reference to the construction of these big ships suggested that the design of their bilge wells might be reconsidered. The idea would be to give them greater capacity and, possibly, more effective ability to get rid of water likely to drain into them – something that was to be expected when carrying ore. Just that: there was no reference to defective welding, to Frame 65, or anything of the sort. How could there have been? The data was on the ocean bed; without it, there could be no theories.

AUTHOR'S NOTE: In the hardback edition of this book, a different story is told about some aspects of the *Derbyshire*. But this was written before the Formal Investigation had been put in hand. In the light of its findings, some of these observations may have been misleading.

9

Ghost Story

The 600-ton freighter *Nannell* may well have had an identity crisis. The point at issue, however, is whether she also had a ghost. This small slut of the high seas used to be called the *Dionissios K* and was registered in Cyprus – a country not noted for its high shipping standards. In 1985 she was bought by a firm of scrap metal merchants. Her name was changed and she was re-registered in Honduras. Her first job should have been to transport twenty-eight miles of surplus cable from Southampton to a port in Kent. But the matter was not quite so simple as that. First of all, the Department of Transport found flaws in her documents, which did not conform to the Merchant Shipping Act. Then there were doubts about her seaworthiness. And, then again, there was uncertainty about what, precisely, was the purpose of her new life. Was she really to be used to carry cargoes of scrap from place to place – or was she intended, as some suggested, for a very different role? According to this school of thought, she was destined to be moored somewhere off the Kentish coast, crewed by robust disc jockeys transmitting popular music. In this capacity, she would become known as station 'Stereo 531'.

All these matters took time to unravel, and the *Nannell* remained at her berth in Southampton. Her new owners denied that they proposed to use her as a pirate radio station. But they also implied that, if anyone wished to buy her for such a purpose, they might be open to offers. Meanwhile, with ten men on board, one woman, and one or two children, she patiently waited for whatever the future might have in store for her.

Meanwhile, in November 1985, there were reports that the idle hands in the idle ship were being bothered by a ghost. The apparition was said to be a slim figure wearing a boiler suit who, mostly at night (though he was sometimes glimpsed in daylight), slipped furtively along the ship's alleyways. Now and again, when those on board her were trying to get a good night's sleep, the spectre went up on deck and kicked up something of a racket. British members of the crew did not seem eager to talk about these visitations. However, one of them confessed to a newspaper reporter that: 'It gives you an uncomfortable feeling from time to time, although he doesn't seem to want to harm us. We've no idea what it could be because we know nothing about the history of the ship.' And, from another: 'It doesn't scare me, but it interests me because I want to know what it is.' A third member was less sanguine. He pointed out that, when he first came aboard, there was a good deal of garlic hanging about. As everyone knows (or ought to), garlic is used to ward off evil spirits (eaten excessively, it is apt to ward off physical bodies as well). Most of these pungent roots had since been removed from the ship, but this man said, 'I've still got one in my room and there's no way I'm taking it down.'

Things seemed to have reached such a pretty pass that the port chaplain was called in. He was unsure of what to do, for he could not recall any similar situation occurring in Southampton. But he promised to convey details of the sightings to the Bishop of Winchester's adviser on exorcism. Perhaps he might be able to make some suggestions.

Eventually, the matter of the *Nannell*'s papers was cleared up and she was allowed to put to sea. She did not remain there for very long: the turbochargers on her diesel engines produced problems, and she had to turn back for repairs. At last, in February 1986, she was judged to be fit for active service and she really did depart. Rumours about her intended role as a pirate radio station persisted – especially since her destination had been changed. It was no longer some port on the coast of Kent, but Pasajes in Northern Spain. There, it was suggested, her crew would spend three weeks fitting the necessary transmitting equipment.

Did the boiler-suited ghost sail with her? No. It transpired that there had never been any such thing. The supposedly unquiet spirit was no more than a product of the crew's imagination, a hoax conceived to while away what must have been a rather tedious period of waiting.

Thus the story of the haunted *Nannell* was reduced to a non-story, and you may consider this account to have been a waste of time. But it may serve to show how cautiously one must treat tales of the supernatural. It is, I must admit, the only item in this small collection of ghost accounts for which I have been able to discover a rational explanation. Some I simply do not believe, and nor, perhaps, will you. But I cannot prove beyond all reasonable doubt that they are false.

One of which I am extremely sceptical concerns the famous Cunarder *Queen Mary*, now spending her declining years as an hotel and tourist attraction at Long Beach California. Big spenders can avail themselves of the luxury of the Winston Churchill Guest Suite. According to three of the suite's occupants, the attractions include a glimpse of the great man himself. He appears long after most people have gone to sleep – standing beside a table, smoking his inevitable cigar, and staring at what he may, perhaps, regard as the intruders. Presently he fades away. If the spirit of Sir Winston were in the habit of making spectral appearances, I can think of all sorts of places that he might decide to haunt, but the *Queen Mary* would not be among them. Nevertheless, those who believe they have seen him have carried sufficient conviction to go on record.

Sir Winston is one of a trio of ghosts that have been seen (or are said to have been seen) in the once magnificent liner. Another, or so it is said, appears on the swimming pool's diving board. She is a woman in early middle-age, wearing a brightly-coloured bathing costume that can fairly be regarded as a period piece from the 'thirties. Although apparently poised for action, she never takes the plunge. Indeed, if you approach her, she instantly disappears.

A woman did, in fact, drown in the pool on some date in the 1930s. Similarly, down in the engine room, a greaser was killed when he was working on the drive-shaft. He, too, reappears, always wearing blue overalls and making himself useful at night. Since the engines are unlikely to function again, this generosity may seem to be unnecessary. But there you are: who knows the motives of the dear departed who have not entirely departed.

The case of the *Port Pirie* suggests a ghost that really did have a purpose – and an important one, too. This motor vessel was built on the Tyne in 1946. Her gross tonnage was 10,500; she had accommodation for a crew of seventy and a dozen first class passengers. Travelling at $16\frac{1}{2}$ knots, she used to ply between Britain, Australia and New Zealand – one of several passenger-cargo liners built in those days, a member of a species that has sadly become extinct.

On a night in 1949 the *Port Pirie* was lying alongside the quay at Sydney. Down in the engine room, the sixth engineer, a young man named Peter Jones, was working in one of the main engine's crank cases. The donkeyman, who was responsible for the auxiliary boiler, was helping him. At some point, Jones told his companion that his assistance was no longer needed and that he might retire to bed.

The night wore on; Mr Jones carried on with his work until he heard the feed pump, which made sure that the auxiliary boiler contained sufficient water, hammering away for all it was worth. He went over to investigate and saw that the gauge indicated that it was full. He turned the pump off and resumed his labours. Before long, the pump started up again. Again, the gauge recorded 'full' and, again, Mr Jones fixed the pump. This went on for quite some time – until he decided that the matter deserved more detailed investigation. Somewhat to his amazement, he discovered that the gauge was faulty and that, far from being adequately supplied waterwise, the boiler must have been almost empty.

Had the pump not decided to overrule the instructions of himself and of the automatic control, the boiler would have exhausted its contents – with explosive results.

Nowadays, as we all know, computers have taught things to think for themselves and a lot of human activity has become redundant. In those days technology was not so advanced and, just as a dog requires a master, so did mechanical creations. The idea of a thinking pump, which somehow *knew* that its services were required, was highly improbable. But, Mr Jones told himself, this is what had happened. As to the cause of it, he had simply no idea.

At seven o'clock, he came off duty and, after a shave and a change into uniform, he joined his colleagues for breakfast. He told them about the strange incident of the pump in the night. They, being older hands than he was, were less surprised. One of them told him the story of the previous donkeyman. On this occasion, the boiler really had run out of water and really had blown up. The unfortunate individual had been caught by the blast and received fatal injuries. But, before he shuffled off his mortal coil, he vowed that such a thing should never happen again. In the speaker's mind there was no doubt about what had happened. The pump had not suddenly developed an intelligence of its own: the dead donkeyman had returned to duty – seen that the gauge served only to mislead, and activated the machinery.

The next case may be considered a digression. There is no ship involved and, come to that, no ghost. Nevertheless, it seems to fit into these pages as an example of the possibly supernatural. The theme, you might say, is that of the *Mary Celeste* – though it has never attracted anything like so much attention. This is strange. The business of the *Mary Celeste* can be explained by an hypothesis that is convincing even if it doesn't prove anything. The matter of the Flannan light seems to defy all attempts at conjecture.

Flannan Islands (or 'The Seven Hunters' as some people call them) are small chunks of land twenty or so miles to the west of Lewis in the Outer Hebrides. Since they are a potential hazard to shipping, they are equipped with a lighthouse. In 1900 it was attended by three men: the chief keeper (James Ducat), the first assistant (Thomas Marshall), and the super-numerary keeper (Donald McArthur). During the early part of December, there had been a spell of extremely bad weather. Then it moderated. On the 15th a coaster homeward bound for Greenock passed reasonably close to the islands. To the captain's surprise, the light issued no reassuring sweeps. On docking at Greenock, he reported that it was out of action. Through some oversight, the news was not passed on to the Scottish Lighthouse Board.

On Boxing Day, as a matter of routine, the Board's supply ship *Hesperus* visited the islands and anchored offshore. Among other things, a relief keeper named Joseph Moore had to be landed and one of the resident trio taken back to the mainland for a spell of leave. The vessel's anchor had not long been lowered, when one of the officers remarked to the captain that there seemed to be something odd. Normally on such visits, somebody would come out of the lighthouse – to wave a welcome, something like that. On this occasion, however, there was nobody to be seen. The master, Captain Harvey, agreed that this was strange and ordered a recognition rocket to be fired. There was no response.

A boat with Mr Moore on board was dispatched to the shore. The relief keeper went inside and, after a while, came out with a worried look on his face. There was, he reported, nobody there. An investigation showed that a meal had been prepared and set out on the living room table. But it had not been eaten. One of the chairs had been overturned – which might have suggested a hurried departure. But to where? On a Flannan island, there is not very much scope for journeys. The log had been kept up-to-date until the 13th; an adjacent slate, on which notes were made, recorded that the lantern had been lit on the 14th and extinguished on the morning of the 15th. The barometric and thermometer readings for the 15th had also been jotted down. But, after that: nothing.

The official view was that the three men had left the light to rescue some of their fishing gear that was in danger of being snatched away by the heavy seas. While they were about their business, a large wave had swept them into the ocean. More local opinion was doubtful about this. At least one man would have been left behind. In any case, assuming that the records indicated that whatever had happened occurred on the 15th, why bother *then*? The weather had calmed down. The sea was more moderate. Why, for heaven's sake why, worry about such things after the gales were gone? And, finally, what was all this about three men being wiped away by a big breaker? There were no large waves that day.

No convincing solution was ever advanced for the Flannan mystery. However, somebody once pointed out that a keeper on the Inchcape (or Bell) Rock off Dundee did, in 1937, think that he saw a ship in distress. He made his way to the water's edge and then went on walking – and walking, drawn, or so it seemed, into the sea by some magnetic force. The inquiry into his death revealed that there were no ships at all in the vicinity at the time, let alone one in distress. For one man to succumb to some strange spell may not seem impossible. But for three? The proposition does not seem reasonable.

Some vessels are launched into the sea of troubles that persist, on and off, throughout their lives. The problems of a few begin while they are still on the slipways. The German World War I submarine *UB-65* was just such a vessel. Boats in the under-water branch of the Kaiser's navy fell, roughly, into three groups. The U-boat itself could, provided there were replenish-ments of fuel available, go anywhere and, virtually, do anything. The UB series was built for coastal operations, and the UC boats were small minelayers.

The *UB-65* was built at the Vulkan Works, Hamburg, in 1917. When she was still under construction, a heavy girder slipped out of a sling and crashed on to the slipway. One man was killed outright; another was seriously injured. He later died in hospital. When she was nearing completion, toxic fumes filled the engine room. Three more men lost their lives. The fault was put right. The *U-65* was completed and set off for the German-occupied port of Bruges, where she came under the command of Admiral Schroeder.

Before taking part in operations, she had to carry out further trials. They were executed off the Friesian Islands: the weather was moderate, and they should have been little more than a formality. However, as in so much of the *UB-65*'s story, there were a number of disturbing incidents. When the boat was still on the surface, an experienced member of the crew was ordered up front to inspect the forward part of the hull. He walked off on his errand; but, like the lighthouse keeper on Inchcape Rock, he seemed to be drawn towards the sea. He did not slip. He was not washed overboard. He just went on walking until he ran out of submarine and fell into the water. Attempts to recover him failed and he drowned.

When the drama was over, the captain ordered the hatches to be closed and the submarine dived to what should have been a depth of thirty feet. In fact, it was rather deeper, for the small vessel continued to descend until she was on the bed of the North Sea. Water found its way into the hull, reached the batteries, and, gradually, poisonous fumes began to pervade her interior. She lay there for twelve hours until, by what must have seemed to be a miracle, she managed to surface. There were no casualties and she was able to make her way back to Bruges, where she was dry-docked.

But this was not the end of the misfortunes that dogged this luckless vessel. When at last she was deemed fit for active service, the torpedoes had to be loaded on board. The warhead of one of them exploded for no apparent reason at all, killing the second officer and five ratings. Admiral Schroeder ordered her back into dry dock though the damage to the boat was not substantial. Perhaps he, like the *UB-65*'s crew, was beginning to suspect that, among the submarine's complement, there was a jinx.

At last the *UB-65* was ready for her first patrol. She had not been at sea for long, when the petty officer of the watch stumbled into the small wardroom and collapsed at the feet of the first lieutenant. When he had recovered sufficiently to speak, he blurted out, 'The dead man's come aboard'. The 'number one' decided that he was drunk and ordered him to his quarters. But he was not drunk: another man, a rating named Pedersen, had also seen the apparition and he was more articulate.

Pedersen, it transpired, had been standing on the deck at the foot of the conning tower, when he saw a strange figure standing in the bows. His arms were folded and he was staring fixedly along the length of the boat. When asked whether he could identify him, Pedersen was in no doubt at all. It was, he insisted, the late second officer – the victim of that all too explosive torpedo.

The commanding officer interviewed both men, and then called a meeting of his officers. The matter, he said, must have a rational explanation. It was either a practical joke in singularly bad taste, or else it was a masquerade perpetrated by British secret agents and intended to undermine the morale of U-boat crews. Whichever the case, nobody was to utter a word about it. Anyone that did would be put under close arrest.

A couple of days later, when the vessel had returned to Bruges, Pedersen deserted. Before leaving, he told a friend that, in his mind, there was no doubt that the *UB-65* and all her crew were doomed.

On her next patrol, the *UB-65* was rather more successful. She torpedoed a British merchant ship off the coast of Kent. However, when she surfaced fifteen miles off Portland Bill to recharge her batteries, there was another disturbing manifestation. After his death at Bruges, the body of the second officer had been taken to the naval cemetery at Wilhelmshaven, where it was buried with military honours. But now, on this stretch of sea not many miles from the Dorset coast, it reappeared. The starboard look-out saw it first. He cried out and then fainted. On this occasion, there were no accusations of drunkenness by the first officer for he, too, saw it. As before, the dead man was standing in the bows, his arms folded and with no expression on his face. But now he began to walk towards the conning tower until he was a few feet away. Then, as suddenly as he had materialised, he disappeared. Soon afterwards, the captain gave the order to dive.

The voyage back to Bruges took three days. On the way, the *UB-65* sank a British supply ship on passage to Plymouth and crippled another by gunfire. This, so far as the German navy was concerned, was the good news. The bad bit came later, shortly after the boat had docked. An air raid was in progress over the Belgian port – the bombs directed at the U-boat pens. Nobody was certain whether it was the result of a bomb or of a splinter from an anti-aircraft shell. But whatever it was, it performed its deadly work just as the commanding officer was coming ashore. With horrible precision, it decapitated him. Minutes – it may have been seconds – later, one of the ratings saw the second officer's ghost on the *UB-65*'s forward end. As now appeared to be his habit, his arms were folded; his face impassive; his gaze concentrated upon who could tell what.

News of these weird happenings reached the ears of Admiral Schroeder, who treated them seriously. Accompanied by the commodore in charge of U-boats, he paid a visit to the small vessel, cross-examined the crew in some detail, and then sent them home on leave. In their absence, and on the admiral's instructions, a Lutheran chaplain went aboard the boat and carried out a service of exorcism.

For the *UB-65*'s new commanding officer, Admiral Schroeder chose a veteran U-boat hand, Oberleutnant Schelle. Schelle was a no-nonsense character who had little time for the supernatural. On his first trip, it looked as if his firm control (or was it the service of exorcism?) was effective. At all events, the submarine accounted for several Allied ships and there were no reports of any hauntings. However, the seeds of fear had been planted in the lower deck. As a chief petty officer wrote home, 'We were never a pack of nervous fools, but we have known from the first day we served in this ship that there was something evil about her.' He recalled an occasion when the ghost of the second officer had entered his quarters, walked to the far end, and then passed through a bulkhead into the forward torpedo room. He remembered noticing the original commander looking over his shoulder and then, seeing something that he, personally could not see, suddenly trembling. Afterwards he had mentioned it to the captain's steward. Yes, the man said: the late co had definitely believed the *UB-65* to be haunted. He had once remarked upon it. So far as the steward was concerned, it was a by no means friendly spirit and that explained why the unfortunate officer had literally lost his head during the air raid.

The next patrol was to take the *UB-65* farther afield – along the length of the English Channel, southward down the Bay of Biscay, and so to a point off Cape Finisterre where, with other submarines, she was to lie in ambush for a reported Allied convoy. The outward voyage was uneventful; but, then off Finisterre, a lot of things went wrong. The first man to encounter the ghost of the second officer was the leading gunner, a man named Eberhardt. He was in such an emotional state that he had to be given morphine. Possibly the dose was not sufficiently strong. At all events, Eberhardt committed suicide.

Later that night the engineer lieutenant saw it. He fell over, broke his leg, and developed a high fever. Shortly after dawn, the submarine surfaced to recharge her batteries. Petty Officer Richard Meyer was in the conning tower. For no apparent reason, he suddenly climbed down on to the deck and jumped into the sea. Meyer was last seen swimming away from the boat as if all the demons in hell were on his tail. He had to be presumed drowned. The *UB-65* returned to her hiding place beneath the surface.

As expected, the convoy came into range after darkness. The attack went ahead, and the escort ships replied by dropping depth charges. While all this was going on, one of the seamen cried out that he had seen a ghost and then seemed to go mad.

Schelle fired his revolver at him. There is no record of whether the man was injured, but there was no doubt that morale in the *UB-65* was in a very low state – so low, that Schelle decided to disengage from the operation and put back to Bruges. When he went before Admiral Schroeder, he confessed that, sceptic though he might be, he himself had twice seen the second lieutenant's ghost. The admiral, possibly becoming weary of this troublesome submarine, ordered him to be replaced and the boat to be again drydocked.

Schroeder's reasoning is sometimes hard to follow. So far as anyone could tell, there was nothing wrong with the *UB-65* – physically, at all events. The malaise was of a more spiritual nature, and it is difficult to see how a spell out of the water could be expected to cure that. Perhaps it was a last resort. Where exorcism had failed, when a normally very sensible officer asserted that he had seen spectres, what else was there to do?

The story now moves away from the *UB-65* – to the United States submarine *L-2*. On 10 July 1918 the USS *L-2* was at periscope level off Cape Clear on the south-eastern corner of Ireland. Not very far away, a U-boat was on the surface, rolling in the swell. So far as the commander of the *L-2* could see, she appeared to have nobody on board. She might even have been a derelict. But this was no reason to ignore her, and he prepared to attack. It was unnecessary. Without any assistance from the *L-2*, the enemy vessel suddenly exploded from within. Just before she sank, the American submarine's captain caught a glimpse of a young officer standing in her bows, his arms folded, and his eyes staring fixedly at the conning tower. He could have sworn that he had not been there when he first sighted the U-boat.

All the thirty-four officers and ratings in the *UB-65* perished. Appropriately, the last to go was the second officer's ghost. As to the cause of the explosion that caused the boat to self-destruct, it can only be a matter of guesswork – though it seems possible that a torpedo had become jammed in its tube and was detonated by another.

HMS *Asp* had begun her life as the paddle steamer *Fury*, a mail packet serving on the Portpatrick–Donaghdee run. Built in 1815, she was a small ship, not very comfortable, but tolerably reliable and well able to carry out the services that her owners, the Post Office, required of her. For twenty-two years, she plodded across the Irish Sea until, in 1837, she was offered to the Admiralty. Her name was changed to *Asp* and she was assigned to survey work. A lieutenant named George Manley Alldridge was appointed captain. She was Alldridge's first command. By a coincidence, he, too, had been born in 1815.

Before assuming her new role, the *Asp* was handed over to the Pembroke Naval Dockyard for a complete overhaul and whatever modifications had to be carried out. Once, during a conversation with the superintendent, Alldridge was told, 'This ship you've got yourself is haunted, but I don't expect anyone told you.' Alldridge confirmed that nobody had. Later on, another official remarked, 'Do you know, sir, your ship is said to be haunted? I doubt very much if you will get any of the dockyard men to work on her much longer.' Sure enough, not long afterwards, the shipwrights approached him in a body. They, too, said that the *Asp* was haunted. Indeed, they begged him to give her up. It would, they warned, bring him nothing but bad luck.

Lieutenant Alldridge was a down-to-earth young man who was suitably sceptical about the supernatural and was anxious to get on with his new job. A little impatiently, he told them, 'I don't care for ghosts, and I dare say I shall get her to rights fast enough.' This, up to a point, was true. HMS *Asp* assisted in the laying of the first submarine telegraph cable between Holyhead and Dublin, and then spent something like twenty years surveying the approaches to Liverpool and a long stretch of the Welsh coast.

Nevertheless, the men at the dockyard had been right: the *Asp* was indeed the occasional scene of supernatural happenings. Possibly because he recalled his professed scepticism, possibly because he felt that people might laugh at him, whatever the reason George Alldridge kept quiet about the very strange experiences he endured during his service with the ship. However, word of them got out and, some years after he had assumed command, a reporter from the *Pembroke Guardian* asked him for an interview. He replied that he was not prepared to talk to the press. On the other hand, and having thought matters over carefully, he agreed to write an account of the occurrences. It was a long document, meticulous in its detail, and, coming from such a man, disturbingly convincing. He wished, he stressed, that he could find some natural cause for the phenomena: goodness knows, he had tried hard enough, but he had failed.

Alldridge, it seemed, had been having trouble with his eyes. To rest them, he had formed the habit of sitting in his cabin after tea while his second-in-command read aloud to him. Outside the door, there was a space in which a companion ladder gave access to the deck. On the far side, at the after end of the ship, there was another room. During the *Asp*'s life as a mail packet, it had been set aside for the exclusive use of female passengers.

On several occasions, the readings had been interrupted by noises coming from the other cabin. They sounded as if somebody inside it was drunk and staggering about. Alldridge at first assumed that the offender was his steward. He called out, 'Don't make such a noise in there' and they ceased. But when the reading was resumed, the din started up all over again. He repeated his demand for silence; and, again, there was a hush. This repetition of events went on for several minutes – until, feeling that some more drastic action was required, the other officer picked up a lamp and went to investigate. He returned quickly, and Alldridge remarked that he looked strained. But – no: the room was empty. Perhaps it was, but the outbreaks of noise continued without respite. Eventually Alldridge decided that there must be somebody, either drunk or of unsound mind, in the other room. His companion couldn't have searched thoroughly enough. With ill-concealed impatience, he rose from his chair and went to see for himself. He looked everywhere and found nobody. The source of the uproar remained a puzzle.

The *Asp* was anchored in the River Dee, with the coast of Cheshire on one side and Flint on the other. One Sunday, Alldridge was invited to tea by a friend who lived in Queens-ferry. His second-in-command accompanied him. They spent an enjoyable evening and it was about ten o'clock by the time they returned to the ship. As they descended the ladder to Alldridge's cabin, they heard somebody hurrying from one room into the other. 'Stand quite still,' Alldridge said. 'I think we have caught whoever it is.'

Judging from the sound, the trespasser had run from the captain's cabin into the former preserve of lady passengers. Stealthily, the young commanding officer went into his quarters and removed his sword, which was hanging from the bulkhead by his bunk. He handed it to his friend with the instruction, 'Let no one get by.' Then he struck a light and pushed his way into the after cabin. He felt certain that he'd find a man there. He was wrong. As on the previous occasion, the room was deserted.

Every effect must have a cause; every problem, a solution. Such was Alldridge's conviction and these strange goings-on worried him. Nor did the situation improve. The repertoire varied. On some occasions, it seemed as if seats and lockers were being banged about – on others, that glass decanters and tumblers were being clashed together. There was the sound of drawers opening and closing; a washstand rattled; somebody seemed to be pulling out a bed. And yet the room was empty: not only of people, but of all furniture. Had it not been for the fact that his brother officer was also privy to this strange secret of HMS *Asp*, Alldridge might have decided that his imagination was deceiving him – or, to put it more bluntly, that he was going out of his mind.

One night when the ship was at anchor, everything seemed to be quiet in the after cabin. Alldridge was settling himself for what might, at last, be a decent night's sleep, when the quartermaster knocked on his door. Could he come up on deck? The look-out had seen something rather unusual. It was indeed unusual. A woman was standing on the starboard paddle box, pointing to the sky with one finger. Presently she dissolved into the night, and that seemed to be that. But it was not. She was observed on several other occasions – always in the same posture with one finger pointing to the sky.

A while later, the *Asp* was moored in the river not far from Haverfordwest. It was a Sunday. Alldridge had gone ashore to church. Possibly with less spiritual purposes in mind, the rest of the crew had been allowed into the town. Only one man remained on board: his steward.

When he returned to the ship, Alldridge wrote, 'I found his appearance so altered . . . that I scarcely knew the man.' It transpired that, as he was descending the companion ladder, somebody had spoken to him. Voices when they emerge from a visible mouth are not necessarily alarming. But when the speaker is invisible, it is quite another matter. Nor was that all: he had, he said, smelt a woman's perfume and heard the strokes of a brush that suggested she was putting her hair in order. The steward had been so terrified that he fainted. Alldridge did his best to allay his servant's fears, but it was no use. The man begged to be discharged from the ship and to be put ashore as soon as possible.

The lady who pointed ever skywards was having a serious effect upon the crew's morale. Some men deserted; others followed the steward's example and pleaded to be excused duty in this obviously haunted vessel. In desperation, Alldridge appealed to a clergyman. The priest came on board, questioned the remaining members of the ship's complement, and decided that (Alldridge's words) 'Some troubled spirit must be lingering about the vessel'. That, one might have reasoned, was fairly obvious. Nor did it do anything to release the 'troubled spirit'. The lady continued to visit the starboard paddle box and the noises in the after cabin showed no signs of diminishing. By this time Alldridge had become reconciled to them. He went so far as to remark that 'I had taken a kind of pleasure in listening to the various sounds.'

But now the phantom's antics became more intimate. On one occasion he was awakened in the night by a hand on the far side of the bedclothes pressing against his leg. He tried to grab it, but there was nothing there. On another, he was aware of a cold hand resting on his forehead. Again, there was sensation without substance.

In 1857 HMS *Asp* was judged to be in need of repairs and she returned to the naval dockyard at Pembroke. She was berthed alongside one of the quays; a sentry was posted nearby to make sure that no unauthorized person went aboard her. On the first night, he was surprised to see the disturbingly familiar sight of the woman on the paddlebox. He was even more astonished when she walked down the gangway and came towards him. He raised his rifle and uttered a challenge. She paid no attention, but seemed, as he put it, to walk 'through' him. In panic, he fled to the guardroom. It may have been unsoldierly conduct, but military training offers no suggestions on how to deal with the supernatural.

With his courage sufficiently restored and reinforced by two more men, he followed the woman to the graveyard of a ruined church. Rather theatrically, she mounted one of the tombstones and stood there for a while, pointing, as always, one finger to the sky. Then she vanished. Afterwards, there were no more sightings of her, and no more weird noises at the after end of the *Asp*.

But Lieutenant Alldridge was not prepared to leave matters at that. There had to be some sort of explanation of why the phantom had decided to take up residence in his ship. As he had been in charge of her ever since the navy had acquired her, there were no clues to be found in the vessel's life as HMS *Asp*. Consequently, he directed his research to the days when she had been the packet boat *Fury* plying the Irish Sea. It turned out to be rewarding. The ship had docked at Portpatrick after one of her voyages and the passengers had gone ashore. A stewardess made her way to the ladies' cabin to clean it out. To her terror, she saw a body on one of the sleeping berths. It was that of a beautiful young woman and her throat had been cut. The mystery of who was responsible was never solved; nor was the girl's identity ever discovered. She, Alldridge was in no doubt, had been the phantom on the paddlebox; she the cause of the uproar in the cabin.

HMS *Asp* remained in service until 1881, when she was scrapped at the considerable age of sixty-six. Alldridge lived on until 1905, when he died at Paignton in Devonshire.

None of the stories in this chapter, except the one concerning the *Nannell*, has a rational explanation. All the witnesses, so far as I can tell, have been reliable people – not given to flights of the imagination or to deception. It is hard to dismiss them as rubbish. They, surely, are true mysteries.

10

Less than Innocent

In 1906 Britain built a revolutionary battleship named HMS *Dreadnought*. In terms of speed and armament, she was more impressive than anything, anywhere, that had come off a slipway. Among the many imaginations that were inflamed by this new capital ship concept was that of Kaiser Wilhelm II. If Germany were to remain in the same league as the United Kingdom, she, too, must have such men-of-war. Thus the race began: the giants steamed away from the shipyards, each a symbol of national defiance and each a statistic on an anxiously kept score card. How stood the day? Did British Dreadnoughts outnumber those of the Kaiser's navy, or was the German *Kriegsmarine* a ship or two ahead?

As things turned out, the struggle ended in an enormous anti-climax. Churchill may have remarked (concerning Jutland) that the British Commander-in-Chief, Admiral Sir John Jellicoe, 'was the only man who could lose the War in an afternoon'. But Jellicoe neither won the war nor lost it. Jutland, the only major clash of the big battleships, was no Trafalgar. Nobody was victorious. Five thousand or so men died for very little (as was the whole sorry truth about World War I).

Of far greater significance was the development of a much more humble craft that could be produced by a process not unlike mass production and which, when regarded, gave nobody any great feeling of national pride. In 1914 Britain had been in possession of submarines for a dozen years; Germany, for eight years. Pundits of both navies were apt to regard these little vessels with scepticism. Nevertheless, during the next four years, German U-boats came very close to severing the umbilical cord that attached Britain to America, and to reducing the United Kingdom to a state of near-starvation.

On reflection, it is amazing that the German submarines managed to get away with it for so long. The solution to the problem was a very old one and, indeed, it was already being used so far as the transport of troops was concerned. Unlike merchantmen, they travelled in convoys escorted by small surface ships such as destroyers. Why, then, should not the mercantile marine adopt this method? Some theorists made great play of the havoc that might be wrought if a U-boat managed to penetrate any such concentration of shipping. It was also pointed out that assembling the vessels would cause unacceptable delays: that the speed of passage would be slowed down, that there were not enough destroyers to go round, and so on. Even some master mariners were said to oppose the idea.

In the end, Prime Minister David Lloyd George put his foot down. The argument had gone on for long enough. On 10 May 1917 the first merchant ship convoy sailed from Gibraltar. There were plenty of destroyers available. The production of depth charges was proceeding at a healthy pace and new means of detecting submarines were being fitted to surface warships. The grip was broken. The toll of U-boat casualties sharply increased. As somebody estimated, the average crew of a German submarine could expect to make only six voyages before being wiped out. A force that had once come close to ruling the waves was now reduced to a collection of rusting boats manned by prematurely old young men.

But this was 1917. Until then the merchant ships went their various ways unescorted and a great many of them never reached their destinations. One notion conceived to combat the menace was the Q-ship. Also known as 'decoys' and 'mystery ships', they came in several different guises, but the principle was always the same. You took a merchant ship and, with a good deal of ingenuity, gave it sufficient armament to account for a U-boat. The weaponry was cunningly concealed: a gun might be hidden in what appeared to be a hen coop, in a deck house, anywhere so long as it could not be seen. The crews, very often, were the merchant navy men who normally worked the ships, implemented by a naval officer, who was in supreme command, a gunnery officer, and a number of RN ratings and Royal Marines. In some respects, they were like the old warships of pre-Tudor days. These, you will probably recall, were merchant ships commandeered in times of war. Carpenters erected castles fore and aft for the fighting men. They retained their original personnel – to which were added an army captain, a lieutenant, and a detachment of soldiers. The tarpaulins navigated them to wherever the captain directed – after which, the military took care of the fighting.

So as not to arouse any suspicion, the naval personnel in Q-ships were dressed in the less formal style of the merchant service. It was also important that each vessel should be sited in what might be assumed to be her natural habitat. In other words, you would not find an Atlantic liner patrolling the North Sea or a P & O ship somewhere off the north-west coast of Scotland. For this reason tramp steamers and colliers were ideal – not operating on regular routes, they might be found more or less anywhere. Before going into battle, the decoys flew the red ensign (or, in some cases, neutral colours). Then, as the disguise was ripped away and the guns were seen to be there, the white ensign would be run up.

Deception was everything. In some instances, Q-ships were actually steered into the paths of on-coming torpedoes on the principle that an aged tramp steamer, say, was worth less than a U-boat. If this ruse caused the latter to surface and offer a target, the tramp was expendable. But, in the early days at any rate, this was seldom necessary. U-boat commanders tended to conserve their comparatively modest supply of torpedoes for bigger game – such as liners and warships. Lesser prey could be dispatched by gunfire.

No detail was overlooked in the attempts to lure the enemy into the trap. When, for example, the U-boat opened fire, certain members of the crew would be detailed to go through the motions of abandoning ship. They might even enact a charade of making a mess of launching one of the life boats. Everyone remaining on board was in hiding. The submarine would come closer to investigate and to deliver the *coup de grace*. The art lay in estimating when it had reached a point as near as anyone dare hope. Then, with the range reduced to the minimum, the shoot-out could begin.

The early days of Q-ships were unpromising. Fishing boats, a cross-Channel steamer, even sailing vessels, were secretly transformed, but they failed to attract any U-boats. This may be understandable. There were only about 33 German submarines in existence and their commanders were more concerned with the sinking of warships than with the lesser members of the mercantile marine. On the night of 21–22 September 1914, for example, the *U-9*, commanded by Lieutenant Otto Weddigen, was on patrol off the coast of Holland, when a trio of elderly cruisers – HMS *Aboukir*, HMS *Cressy*, and HMS *Hogue* – was spotted. A torpedo sank the *Aboukir* within twenty-five minutes. *Cressy* and *Hogue* went to search for survivors, presented ideal targets, and were dispatched with no less speed. The cruisers were known as the 'live bait squadron'. They dated back to 1902, and their loss could hardly be described as a major blow to British naval might. However, the 1,400 officers and ratings that died were quite another matter.

Weddigen was to be awarded the Blue Max, Germany's highest award for valour. But he, too, had not much longer to live. On 18 March of the following year, now in command of *U-29*, he was entering the Pentland Firth from the North Sea, when his boat was rammed by HMS *Dreadnought*. It was lost with all hands. Nor, indeed, should he have fared so well and with so little effort in his demolition of the old cruisers. The trouble was that bad weather had compelled the destroyers, which ought to have been keeping them company, to head back to their base at Harwich. The importance of escorts, a prime rule of anti-submarine warfare, had already been established, though nobody seems to have realized it.

So far as merchant ships were concerned, the situation was ambivalent. One of the foremost supporters of a submarine building programme in Britain was Admiral of the Fleet Lord Fisher. Winston Churchill, then First Lord of the Admiralty, was less certain. Not the least of the difficulties, he argued, was the use of them to sink merchantmen. 'I do not believe', he told Fisher, 'that this would ever be done by a civilised power.' That was on 1 January 1914.

In the beginning the matter was left to the discretion of the U-boat commanders, and their attitudes varied. Some sank on sight and to hell with the consequences. Others were more compassionate. The common factor was that they all made a nonsense of Churchill's supposition. Once the idea of blockading Britain had been established, they forgot all about being representatives of a 'civilised power'. As far back as 1512, Henry VIII had produced a code of conduct for attacks on enemy merchant ships. Any warship encountering an unarmed vessel should stop her by firing a shot across the bows. A boarding party would then carry out a search. If the ship belonged to a neutral power, she must be allowed to continue her voyage. If she was hostile, the crew and passengers could be taken as hostages; the vessel and her cargo as prizes. Alternatively, if this was not possible, they could be destroyed. The articles were known as The Cruiser Rules.

Whether U-boat commanders had any knowledge of The Cruiser Rules may be doubtful. Nevertheless, Lieutenant-Commander Feldkircher of the *U-17* seems to have been a model of correctitude. When he sank the steamer *Glitra* on passage from Grangemouth to Stavanger, he gave the master ten minutes in which to abandon ship before sending a party on board to open the seacocks. He then took the *Glitra*'s lifeboats in tow until they were within a reasonable distance of the Norwegian coast. Later, off Barrow-in-Furness, Lancashire, he stopped and scuttled three coasters. In each case, he gave their crews ample time in which to escape.

By contrast, Lieutenant-Commander Schneider was made of much sterner stuff. One day in mid-Channel he happened across the French steamship *Admiral Ganteaume* with 2,500 Belgian refugees on board. Without giving any warning, he fired a torpedo and then made off. By some miracle, only forty people lost their lives.

Lieutenant-Commander Walter Schweiger was another member of the sink-and-be-damned persuasion. Commanding the *U-20*, he, too, was operating in the Channel. In one day, he sank three freighters without giving any notice of his intentions. Two days later, he sighted the 12,000-ton hospital ship *Asturias*. There could have been no doubt of his victim's identity: she was painted white and there were large red crosses on her sides (illuminated at night to avoid any possibility of mistakes). But this did not deter Schweiger. He sank the former liner without compassion and returned to the depths.

In early May 1915 Schweiger and his *U-20* were patrolling the southern approaches to the Irish sea. On the sixth, he encountered the Harrison liner *Candidate*. For whatever reason (and there is no means of finding out), he changed his policy and obeyed The Cruiser Rules. When, however, a boarding party carried out a search, its members found two machine-guns and a six-pounder. The rules clearly stated that, to merit clemency, a vessel had to be *unarmed*. Schweiger had been over generous. Determined not to repeat his mistake, he later sank the *Candidate*'s sister ship, the *Centurion*, without regard to any such niceties.

Nor did he hesitate on the following day when, off the Old Head of Kinsale, he saw the approaching mass of the Cunarder *Lusitania* through his periscope. The matter of the *Lusitania* can be (and is) endlessly debated. Did Schweiger fire one torpedo (as he claimed) or two (as the British Admiralty alleged)? Was, in fact, the liner really destroyed from within by explosives she was carrying – to which the *U-20*'s missile served as a detonator? Did Schweiger believe that the Cunarder was, in fact, an armed merchant cruiser? She had, after all, been built with government money on the understanding that she would assume that role in wartime. Indeed, she was even listed in the 1914 edition of *Jane's Fighting Ships*. Whatever the circumstances, 1,198 people died as a result of the *U-20*'s attack and public opinion, both in America and Britain, was outraged.

On 19 August of that year, the White Star liner *Arabic* was on passage to New York. She had reached a point about sixty miles south of Queenstown (Cobh) when the infamous Lieutenant-Commander Schneider and his *U-24* sighted her. Public opinion played little part in Schneider's life: he was a dedicated destroyer of ships and that, so far as he was concerned, was that. He fired a torpedo without agonizing over ethics, and the *Arabic* sank. Thanks to the well disciplined evacuation of her passengers and crew, there were only 44 casualties out of 429 people on board, but his action did little to improve relations between Germany and the United States.

The area of sea between Ireland and the Scilly Islands seems to have been busy that day. Another U-boat – the *U-27* commanded by Lieutenant-Commander Wegener – was also prowling around in search of prey. On the surface, the Leyland liner *Nicosian* was heading for Avonmouth from Houston, Texas, with a cargo of 800 mules intended for the British and French armies. And, also in the region, there was an apparently harmless collier of about 4,000 tons named the *Baralong*. If her flag and the large signs on her sides were to be believed, she was owned by an American firm.

Wegener had an impressive record. In October 1914 he had sunk the cruiser HMS *Hermes* in the Dover Strait with the loss of 22 lives. *Hermes* had been built in 1900. In 1913 she was fitted with a platform forward of her superstructure and thus became one of Britain's earlier seaplane carriers. However, at the outbreak of war, she reverted to the role for which she had originally been intended. With a complement of about 450, the casualty list was commendably moderate.

Later that autumn *U-27* was operating in the North Sea off the Friesian Island of Borkum. The submarine *E3* fell victim to her. There were no survivors from her crew of 30. Finally, on 11 March 1915, Wegener sank the armed merchant cruiser HMS *Bayano* (5,958 tons – formerly a banana boat owned by Elders and Fyffe) off the coast of Galloway in Scotland. Two hundred men were killed.

Undoubtedly Lieutenant-Commander Wegener had to be accounted an ace and anything calculated to put him out of business was to be welcomed. On that pleasant August day, with the sea completely calm and a bright sun burning down, he had no worries about disposing of the *Nicosian*. His supply of torpedoes was running short, but, in such clement weather, this was the least of his worries. He ordered the Leyland liner to stop: gave her master, Captain Manning, ample time in which to abandon ship, and then sent a boarding party of six men across. Their job was to open the seacocks and send the ship peacefully to her grave.

The apparently harmless tramp *Baralong* played no part in Wegener's calculations: indeed, it was doubtful whether he noticed her at first, for she was hidden from his view by the *Nicosian*'s bulk. His first glimpse of her scruffy profile was when she steamed into sight, flying the international code signal seeking permission 'to save life only'. He assented. His good natured agreement was the last, and the greatest, mistake that Wegener ever made. For, despite her innocent exterior, the

Baralong was by no means as harmless as she seemed. She was, in fact, a Q-ship armed with hidden 12-pounders and depth charges.

In peacetime the *Baralong* went about her business as a collier. Her master, Captain Willie McBride, and her merchant marine crew were still working the ship, but she was now under the overall command of Commander Geoffrey Herbert RN, supported by a gunnery officer, 22-year-old Lieutenant G. C. Steele RNR, Petty Officer Dickinson (who had served under Scott on his Antarctic expeditions), eight naval ratings, and a detachment of twelve Royal Marines under Corporal F. G. Collins.

The *Baralong* was within almost point blank range of the *U-27* before she dropped her disguise, replaced the stars and stripes with the white ensign, and hauled in those massive 20 feet by 25 feet boards on her flanks that emphasised her assumed nationality. In the exchange of fire that followed, the *U-27* only unleashed one round, whilst the Q-ship pumped 34 shots into her victim's hull. It was all over within little more than a minute. The stricken submarine heeled over and sank. Those of her crew that had survived the ordeal by gunfire were struggling for survival in the water. The crewmen from the *Nicosian* eventually returned to their ship, which was taken in tow and some while later arrived at Avonmouth.

At this point, the official story of the action comes to an end. Decorations for gallantry were dished out, the *Baralong*'s crew were rewarded with a 'full grant' of £1,000 – the prize for an established sinking (£300 was paid in cases where the result was unproven). As the naval historian E. Keble Chatterton pointed out in *Q-Ships and Their Story* (1922), 'This great success in the midst of a terrible tale of shipping losses finally convinced the authorities of the value of the Q-ship.' Hitherto, with the merchant navy needing every vessel it could get, the Admiralty had been reluctant to commandeer ships for a project in which it had less than complete faith. Now its attitude changed, and, according to one source, 366 ships were modified for this role. There were certainly some very brave actions – especially by Captain Gordon Campell, who was awarded the Victoria Cross and two DSOs. But, all told, the mystery ships accounted for no more than a dozen U-boats at a time when these denizens of the deep were coming off the production lines in considerable quantities.

Mr Keble Chatterton was a conscientious researcher in the years when, surprisingly, there still seemed to be something glorious about war. His book begins with the sentence 'All warfare is merely a contest'. Whether those who fought on the Somme or at Passchendaele would have agreed with this seems doubtful. And, if they had been able to express opinions, those 5,000 victims of Jutland might have disputed the word 'merely'. There can be no knowing whether Mr Chatterton was aware of the complete story of the *Baralong–U-27* action – or whether, had he been informed of it, he would have used it. He was writing in an age when there were still heroes and the nasty bits were apt to be swept aside. It was almost as if he and his contemporaries were keeping alive the gleaming image of combat – knowing that, before too long, it would be needed again and another generation would have to fight.

The Admiralty must have known the truth, but it kept it well hidden. Even nowadays documents to do with the affair are missing from the Public Record Office; and when, in 1961, an author applied to the Ministry of Defence for permission to inspect the relevant files, he was given assent upon the strict understanding that nothing should be published without official agreement. However word gets around and, before World War I was over, Germany knew about a less savoury aspect of the affair, and so did the United States government. The probable sources were talkative Irish stokers from the *Nicosian* whose homes were in Liverpool.

Up to the point at which the *U-27* foundered, Mr Keble Chatterton's account is more or less correct – although he omitted to mention the signal flown by the *Baralong*, indicating that she was about to pick up survivors. But this was by no means the end of the matter.

We return to the scene moments after the *U-27* had foundered. Instinctively, the German sailors swam in the direction of the *Nicosian*'s lifeboats – never doubting, it appears, that they would be given sanctuary. But Corporal Collins had other ideas. He lined up his Marines on the *Baralong*'s deck and ordered them to open fire. With admirable marksmanship, they picked the men off one by one until there were only two left alive. The survivors reached a pilot ladder that was dangling down the Leyland liner's side. Each was allowed to climb it until his head was level with the deck. Each was then dispatched with a perfectly judged round to join his comrades. The *Nicosian*'s crew gave an approving cheer.

There were now only six members of the U-boat's complement still extant: the boarding party that Wegener had charged with the responsibility for scuttling the merchantman. The ethics of what happened next must depend upon which of two stories you prefer to accept. According to one account, the Germans, bewildered by the turn of events and hoping for compassion, lined up and meekly raised their hands. However, Herbert, recalling the events twenty years afterwards, disputed this. 'Instead of going to a prominent place on the upper deck and holding up their hands in surrender,' he wrote, 'these six darted below and left me no option but to assume they were about to destroy the steamer.'

Was Commander Herbert's memory distorted by the years, or was the place not sufficiently 'prominent' for him to see the men from the *Baralong*'s bridge? Captain McBride, on Herbert's instructions, brought the Q-ship alongside the *Nicosian*: Collins and his detachment of men from the Royal Marine Light Infantry clambered from one vessel to the other. Of that there is no doubt. But now we find the U-boat personnel still on deck – and, indeed, lined up. The corporal wasted no time in conversation. He raised his rifle and promptly shot the nearest German. Afterwards, he boasted of having killed Wegener, though there is no evidence to prove it. But, then again, did he mean that the erstwhile U-boat commander had been his victim on this particular occasion? Perhaps not, for the luckless officer crops up a few minutes later in another recollection.

Once Collins had made his intention clear, the five surviving men did most certainly scatter. Some tried to hide behind winches, some behind hatch coamings, and one attempted to barricade himself in a cabin. When a Marine battered down the door with his rifle butt, the terrified sailor pushed his way past, sprinted across the deck, and dived into the sea – swimming for goodness knows where. But he did not remain afloat for long. Giving a further display of his marksmanship,

Collins discharged another round – which, again, found its mark. This, or so another witness suggested, was Wegener.

But, one has to ask, were either of the identifications correct? It is surely improbable that a submarine captain would have left his command to supervise a task that could have been adequately performed by a subordinate.

Meanwhile, the *Nicosian*'s seamen were returning to their ship. Captain Manning crossed the small gap that separated her from the *Baralong* and made for the latter's bridge. If he is to be believed, he found Herbert in a state of great elation: rubbing his hands together and chortling something about 'Remember the *Lusitania*'. He may also have mentioned the *Arabic*.

Clearly anyone who hopes to win battles must be prepared to kill. But, under the Geneva Convention, anyone who had fought and lost was entitled to mercy. Whether or not the men from *U-27* had formally surrendered seems to make little difference. The fight had gone out of them: they were scared out of their wits and desperate to find a hiding place in which they could remain secure until tempers had cooled. As the events which followed showed, they had every reason to be afraid. If the accounts handed down by word of mouth are true (and one account differs from another only in matters of detail) – if these are a fair summary of what happened, a blood lust stopping only marginally short of insanity appears to have infected representatives of both the *Baralong*'s and the *Nicosian*'s crews.

One of the *U-27*'s men now lay bleeding on deck: four had bolted for the possible safety of the engine room. The Marines followed them, chasing them up the shaft alley and firing indiscriminately. This time (according to one account) their shots went wide of the mark. But, again in this version, it didn't matter. The soldiers were prepared to leave the final act of brutality to the *Nicosian*'s stokers, who set about their task with an unholy zest. The German rating who was probably already dying on deck was taken to join his companions. The four in the shaft alley were rounded up with little difficulty. They were all now manhandled to an ash-chute, where they were tied by their feet and hung upside down. But this was only a beginning. Presently they were cut down, scooped up, and flung into the furnaces where they were burned alive.

In his report on the action, Commander Herbert stated, simply, that 'Searching for Germans who might scuttle the *Nicosian*, a party of Marines found six who succumbed from the injuries they had received from a lyddite shell.' Corporal Collins once said that he was 'not quite sure what happened below' – though he knew well enough what had happened above. But people talk. In an article in the magazine *Sea Breezes*, Mr Fred G. Shaw recalled a story he had once been told by a merchant navy officer. Apparently some weeks after the action this man was having a drink in an Avonmouth hotel, when he fell into conversation with the Leyland liner's third mate. After a few drinks, the latter mentioned that 'a nasty incident' had occurred on the voyage, but he was not allowed to talk about it. Later that evening, when the *Nicosian*'s officer had increased the level of alcohol in his blood, he was more talkative and he described the ghastly sequence of events. In a letter to Mr Shaw, written in 1965, a former ship's officer, Mr G. A. Moller, who had obviously delved into the matter with considerable thoroughness, wrote that 'in spite of the official secrecy, the story was all over Bristol within an hour of the *Nicosian*'s safe arrival – and all over Merseyside soon after'. Indeed, he suggested that the first person to hear of it was a lady working as counter clerk in the main post office at Bristol. Business, it seems, was brisk with *Nicosian* crewmen handing in telegrams that announced their safe arrival. The first person to refer to the matter in print was Rear-Admiral William Jameson in his book about submarine warfare (*The Most Formidable Thing*, published in 1965). But Admiral Jameson trod cautiously. He tended to dismiss what was possibly the truth as little more than rumours.

When the German authorities heard about the atrocity, they lodged a protest in which they blamed the *Baralong*'s Captain McBride for the slaughter. Predictably, the British Government rejected it. Nevertheless, some decisions were taken that suggest either an uneasy conscience – or else that the Germans were not simply fabricating a tale for propaganda purposes, but that they really believed such things had happened.

The *Baralong*'s name was changed to *Wyandra*. For a while, she continued her career as a Q-ship. On 24 September 1915, now commanded by Lieutenant-Commander A. Wilmot-Smith RN, she sank the *U-41* off the Scilly Islands. But, on this occasion, there were no subsequent suggestions of unpleasantness. Indeed, the U-boat's commander and the helmsman were both saved. Nevertheless, reminded of the *U-27*'s fate, the German authorities were quick to protest. Not long afterwards, they insisted that captured Q-ship personnel would be treated as pirates and shot. This may seem to have been a foretaste of Hitler's *Kommandobefehl* directive in World War II, in which he ordered that Commando 'sabotage parties and their accomplices will be ruthlessly exterminated in battle by German troops . . . Should it prove advisable to spare one or two men in the first instance for interrogation reasons, they are to be shot immediately after their interrogation.' The difference was that Hitler meant what he said: there is no evidence to suggest that the threat to the Q-ship crews was ever carried out.

Later in the war, the *Baralong* (or *Wyandra*) was stripped of her armament and used as a fleet ammunition ship. In 1922 she was sold to Japanese owners and she was still flying the Nippon flag in 1933, when she went to the shipbreakers.

More significantly, perhaps, the *Nicosian*'s name was also changed – to *Nevisian*. What is more, her crew were issued with new discharge books in which all references to the voyage in August 1915 were omitted. Some of them even went to the extent of altering their own names. Mr Moller, who made two consecutive voyages in her as an apprentice in 1923, recalled that bullet holes could still be seen in the shaft alley. To judge by his account, she does not seem to have been a happy ship. On the first trip the chief officer went mad and let go the anchor in mid-Atlantic. It took 18 days to travel from Liverpool to Boston, with the vessel beset by blizzards for much of the way. Three days out from Liverpool, one of the engineers died. He was buried at sea; but, at the first attempt, the sea appeared to reject him. A wave slung the body back on deck, partly destroying the canvas shroud and causing the dead man's head to stick out. The second attempt was more successful.

On Mr Moller's next trip, the vessel was berthed in New York, when she was unexpectedly ordered to proceed to Hamburg. A number of hands had been in her during the encounter with *U-27* and the news caused several of them to desert. Unlike the situation in Britain, the incident had received wide coverage in Germany and they feared reprisals. As things turned out, their misgivings were unfounded. Faced with rampant inflation and severe shortages of food, the citizens of Hamburg were more concerned with getting something to eat than in settling past scores.

Commander Herbert died in 1961. Corporal Collins has probably followed him by now. The whereabouts of the rest, assuming they are still alive, is unknown and the *Nicosian* /*Nevisian* has long been scrapped. The truth of that dreadful day in August 1915 must remain, legally at any rate, a matter of speculation. Indeed, Mr Shaw's article in *Sea Breezes* was followed up by a reader's letter referring to Dr Carson I. A. Richie's book *Q-Ships*.

According to Dr Richie, Collins did indeed hunt down the Germans and shot them 'in default of surrender' – which may suggest that they did not, in fact, line up with their hands aloft. This, apparently, was on the instructions of Commander Herbert, who was afraid that they might have armed themselves with rifles taken from the *Nicosian*'s chart room. Herbert warned that they were desperate men likely to open fire at no matter what cost. On the evidence of Dr Richie, Wegener had not sent them from the U-boat as a boarding party; but, in fact, they were survivors who managed to reach the possible sanctuary of the ship after the submarine had foundered and despite the rifle fire of the Marines. Dr Richie remarks that 'the story of the *Baralong* lost nothing in the telling . . . it had become part of the folklore of the First World War.'

Perhaps it did, but a key witness, Lieutenant-Commander Wegener was unable to testify. Without his evidence, and whether you accept the hypothesis of Dr Richie or that of Messrs Shaw and Miller, you are on uncertain ground. It would have been sensible to conserve torpedoes and to scuttle the merchant ship so why not do it? If those six sailors managed to board the *Nicosian* after the *U-27* had sunk, how did they know that there were rifles in the chart room? And, having armed themselves, what did they propose to do? Half a dozen men would not have been sufficient to work this 4,000-ton vessel: hardly enough, indeed, to maintain a head of steam from her boilers. Did they intend to shoot as many people as possible – and then to die gloriously for the Fatherland by opening the seacocks? Did Commander Herbert assume that this was what they had in mind?

Neither the Richie nor the Shaw/Moller factions leave us in any doubt that the few who survived the submarine's destruction were killed. The two points at issue are whether the slaughter was justified, and whether the *Nicosian*'s firemen did indeed burn the Germans alive. On both counts there seems to be too little evidence to record a verdict. One would dearly like to believe that the stokers were not guilty of such appalling inhumanity. On the other hand, they were clearly in an excitable frame of mind. They had also lost many of their friends in U-boat actions against other British merchantmen. Were they, then, able to resist this opportunity for a kind of symbolic revenge? It is, perhaps, doubtful.

Whatever your views, it has to be conceded that there was something mysterious about the *Baralong–U-27* business – a mystery that, at this distance in time can never be solved.

11

The Ice Ship

Lake Patricia in Canada is a lonely place and, in winter, extremely cold. Nor is the nearby town of Jasper a model of the modern metropolis. To be honest, it does not amount to very much. Nevertheless, anyone who wandered down to the edge of the water during the winter of 1943–4 must have been puzzled. A small settlement of buildings had suddenly sprung up – and there, close inshore, was a large object that could at first have been mistaken for an iceberg. However, a thoughtful observer might presently have had doubts about this. A berg is something that snaps off the end of a glacier and deposits itself in the sea. There is no sense of design about its appearance: nothing that prompts the onlooker to say, 'Ah – this is a standard model of such-and-such a year' or anything like that.

This berg was too regular in its shape to be attributed to the haphazard, free-hand, style of nature. It looked as if it had originated on a drawing board. (Nature seems to abhor straight lines: man rather likes them.) But this was not its only peculiarity. As winter turned to spring, and spring to summer, this strange intruder did not succumb to the thaw that softened the surrounding countryside. It was, to anyone who didn't know the story behind it, quite a puzzle.

At one minute to midnight GMT on Thursday, 28 February 1946, a press release – issued simultaneously from London, Washington and Moscow – made everything clear. The oddity had indeed been a human invention; the reason why it did not melt was that it was not composed entirely of ice. To be sure, 86 per cent of its volume was frozen water, but the remaining 14 per cent was wood pulp. The substance was known as Pykrete after its inventor, Geoffrey Pyke.

Mr Pyke was one of the stranger characters to appear on the stage of World War II. He had no qualifications for work as a creator of unusual materials and none as a naval architect. Indeed, when he attended Pembroke College, Cambridge, just before the First World War, he read law. This was not perhaps surprising: his father was a solicitor and it was unremarkable that he should have decided to follow Pyke Senior's profession. But he never practised. When the war was still young, he managed to persuade the *News Chronicle* to appoint him as its German correspondent. Using a forged American passport, he made his way to Berlin via Sweden and diligently reported events as best he could. He took little trouble to maintain his cover and, before very long he was arrested as a spy. For a while, as he languished in solitary confinement, it looked as if, on one early morning or another, he might be shot. But the authorities relented. Instead, he was taken to the civilian internment camp at Ruhleben (not far from Berlin) from which, in 1915, he escaped to Holland.

There were some people who described Geoffrey Pyke as a 'genius' and one doubts whether he would have disputed it. Intellectually, his ideas were always original and sometimes outrageous. There was a certain arrogance about his manner: too much, really, to make him socially acceptable. He sported a shaggy goatee beard on his chin; regarded the world thoughtfully through a pair of lightweight horn-rimmed spectacles; and displayed a well judged contempt for the more conventional ideas about how to dress. Indeed, a man might have been forgiven had he mistaken Mr Pyke for an earnest looking tramp.

Between the wars, he dabbled in high finance; worked at the Malting House School in Cambridge, where they practised the scientifically controlled education of young children; and even wrote advertising copy for Shell (but, in those days, the oil company encouraged the talents of slightly eccentric young men: the Company Man had not yet completely taken over).

Whether Geoffrey Pyke's judgement was entirely sound could be a matter for debate. There was, however, one occasion on which he undoubtedly got things right. That was in 1942, when Mountbatten was appointed Chief of Combined Operations. Without bothering to spruce himself up, Mr Pyke presented himself at the headquarters of combined ops with an introduction from Leo Amery, Secretary of State for India. Despite his unpromising appearance, he managed to obtain an audience. His first words were, 'Lord Mountbatten, you need me on your staff because I am a man who thinks'. When he had listened to him for a while, Mountbatten was inclined to agree with him. He appointed him Civilian Director of Programmes.

It had not escaped Mr Pyke's notice that a large proportion of Europe (he put it at 70 per cent) is snowbound for five months of the year. This gave him the idea that a small force, say a thousand men, could pin down 250,000 German soldiers if it had sufficient mobility and was experienced enough in winter warfare. The mobility would come from a lightweight tracked vehicle of his invention, which he called the 'Weasel' (later known as M29). The cold weather experience would be achieved by recruiting the men from Canadian and United States forces. Ingeniously, the Weasel was so constructed that it could be carried to its destination in a Lancaster bomber.

Thus Operation Plough was conceived and described in a 54-page memorandum. Mountbatten liked it: the Royal Air Force was less impressed. Every serviceable Lancaster, some senior officer pointed out, was needed for the bombing offensive against Germany. There was none to spare for carting small vehicles of unproven reliability about the sky. However the US Army's Chief of Staff, General George Marshall, was taken with the idea in principle. As a result, the 1st US-Canadian Special Force was created. It was variously known as 'the North Americans' and 'The Black Devils' (from a letter found in the pocket of a dead German soldier, which remarked that 'The black devils are all around us every time we come into the line and we never hear them'). It was certainly one of the most brave, brutal, and brigandly units ever to fire shots in anger.

Meanwhile, the ingenious Mr Pyke had directed his thinking to another topic. The inspiration must have come from the efforts of the International Ice Patrol (run by the US Coast Guard) in its war against icebergs. From time to time, the patrol had fired shot and shell at wandering bergs, and even attempted to demolish them by carefully placed charges of high explosive. It had all been in vain: these super strong creations of nature seemed to shrug off the attacks as a human being suffers no more than short lived inconvenience from an intrusive fly. Nevertheless, they have a weakness. Drifting, say, from the cold waters of the Labrador Current into the warmer Gulf Stream, they melt.

The problem, then, was to delay this process. After experiments assisted by the National Physical Laboratory at Teddington and the Cold Storage Laboratory in London, he discovered that the addition of wood pulp not only prolonged the process considerably, it also toughened the ice. He called the product Pykrete and decided that, in certain applications, it would provide a very acceptable substitute for steel. This, surely, was to be welcomed: in war-beleaguered Britain, there was never enough steel. In a way, it was a kind of liberation. With this comparatively easily made substance at his disposal, his always fertile imagination could work without restraint. He envisaged freighters 80 times as large as Liberty ships, which were the wartime workhorses of the ocean, and aircraft carriers. The latter could be used as bases for anti-submarine warfare in the North Atlantic, and as miniature aerodromes to cover Allied landings on the coast of Europe. Bombs and torpedoes were robbed of their menace. They could pierce steel without very much difficulty. In the case of Pykrete, they would do little more than produce small craters that could easily be filled in. He had, now that he came to think of it, come very near to devising the really unsinkable ship. Only time could destroy it and that would be a very leisurely process. There is no evidence to suggest that he recalled the case of the *Titanic*; but, if he did, he must have found a nice irony in the proposition that the killer of the reputedly indestructible should provide the inspiration for something that might very nearly live up to that description.

Having found his raw material, Mr Pyke applied himself to designing a use for it. He planned to build an aircraft carrier of two million tons (26 times the displacement of the liner *Queen Elizabeth*), two thousand feet long, 300 feet broad, and 200 feet deep. It would be capable of withstanding waves 1,000 feet long and 50 feet tall, and its hangars would provide accommodation for 200 Spitfire fighters or 100 Mosquito bombers. A diesel electric system of power would give it a speed of seven knots (which he judged to be more than sufficient) and a range of about 7,000 nautical miles. Three hundred and thirty-four officers would serve in her, 40 warrant officers, 164 petty officers, and 3,052 ratings – making a total of 3,590.

By contrast, HMS *Indefatigable*, Britain's largest aircraft carrier of those days, displaced 23,000 tons, was 766 feet long, had a speed of 30 knots, accommodation for 60 aircraft, and carried a complement of about 2,000 officers and men.

Pyke named his massive idea HMS *Habbakuk* (students of the Old Testament will notice that it is a misspelling: the prophet in question was Habakkuk. There was nothing intentional about this. It was a typing error by his secretary which he never bothered to correct). The appropriate lines were: 'Behold ye among the heathen, and regard, and wonder marvellously: for I will work a work in your days, which ye will not believe, though it be told you.' Actually, Pyke always said that he was thinking of a character likewise named in Voltaire's *Candide*, who could achieve anything he wanted. But never mind: the wrongly spelt name stuck and people could believe whatever they wanted.

The 54-page memorandum for 'Plough' was short by comparison with the length to which Pyke went to explain *Habbakuk*. It required 232 pages of foolscap or 55,000 words – the length of a shortish novel. When the manuscript arrived on Mountbatten's desk, the Head of Combined Operations might have been forgiven if he had dismissed it as too long – and handed it to an underling. But Pyke knew his man. Mountbatten was fond of reading about the exploits of G. K. Chesterton's priest/detective Father Brown. In chapter seven of *The Scandal of Father Brown* ('The Point of a Pin'), we read: 'Father Brown laid down his cigar and said carefully: "It isn't that they can't see the solution. It is that they can't see the problem."' The quotation appeared at the very beginning and captured Mountbatten's attention. He was also invited to throw the document away if, after half an hour, he had become bored with it. Mountbatten did not become bored: indeed the apparently outrageous concept appealed greatly to his enjoyment of originality. Whether it appealed to a luckless scientist who, later on, was instructed to extract the essence of the idea and to put it down on one sheet of paper – that is another matter.

Lord Mountbatten, then, could be accounted an early enthusiast for *Habbakuk*. But other people had to be sold on it – particularly Winston Churchill. The Prime Minister was staying at Chequers at the time and, by a happy chance, Mountbatten had been invited to dine with him. He took with him two containers: one packed with ice, the other with a sample of Pykrete. When he arrived, he was told that Churchill was taking a bath. What better opportunity could there be? He hurried up to the bathroom and, after a few words of explanation, emptied both containers into the hot water. The ice melted; the Pykrete did not. (The demonstration performed in front of President Roosevelt was rather less informal: two silver soup tureens filled with warm water were produced for the performance.)

Churchill was excited about the proposition. In a rather more public place he said:

> I attach the greatest importance to the examination of these ideas. The advantages of a floating island, or islands, if only used as refuelling depots for aircraft, are so dazzling that they do not at the moment need to be discussed . . . The scheme is only possible if we let nature do nearly all the work for us and use, as raw material, sea water and low temperature. The scheme will be destroyed if it involves the movement of very large numbers of men and heavy tonnage of steel or concrete to the remote recesses of the Arctic night.

This, of course, was only the beginning. The extra toughness of Pykrete also had to be shown. At its simplest, a block of ice was smashed with a hammer; a block of Pykrete underwent the same ordeal and survived. A nail was knocked into ice. It failed to penetrate Pykrete. But the most dramatic demonstration – theatrical, indeed – took place at the Ottawa Conference in early 1943. The Combined Chiefs of Staff were assembled. A lump of ice was produced and then a lump of Pykrete. Armed with a borrowed revolver, Mountbatten, who was a very fair shot, put one round into the ice, which disintegrated. Then he loosed off at the Pykrete. The bullet smacked it, bounced off, did minor damage to a leg belonging to the American Chief of Naval Operations, and came to rest in one of the walls. Outside, the staff officers became concerned. Were their masters in such great disagreement that their business had degenerated into a shoot-out?

Pyke followed the progress of his brainchild with some anxiety. In *Mountbatten*, Philip Ziegler quotes Solly Zuckerman, then scientific adviser to Combined Operations HQ. The only begetter of *Habbakuk* had, it appears, been ill and was now recovering at his apartment in Albany (that very exclusive residence in Piccadilly: it must have made a nice change from the inter-war years, which were conspicuous for Pyke's lack of affluence). 'Pyke was sitting up, looking with his strange beard, like some jaundiced Christ', Zuckerman wrote. 'Mountbatten tried to assure him that work was proceeding as fast as it possibly could. Pyke was not satisfied. "Without faith", he kept protesting, "nothing will come of this project." "But I have faith," replied Mountbatten. "Yes," said Pyke, "but have others got faith?", and turning to Harold Wernher he asked solemnly: "Have you got faith, Brigadier?" Poor Wernher did not know what to say, but before he could utter a word, the C.C.O. had chipped in with the remark: "Wernher's on my staff, to see that I am not over-lavish with my own faith."' (Wernher's job was to arrange supplies of material and labour for Combined Operations.)

There were a number of other individuals and agencies ready to protect Mountbatten against himself. Professor Frederick Lindemann (later Lord Cherwell), Churchill's chief scientific adviser, had so little confidence in the venture that he refused to sit on the committee appointed to examine its feasibility. The Americans, who would have to provide such steel as was necessary, were sceptical. In Britain, the First Lord of the Admiralty, A. V. Alexander, agreed with the Americans; and, when he realized that it would cost rather more than Pyke had estimated and Mountbatten had suggested, Churchill's interest began to flag.

Nevertheless, the Chiefs of Staff were not unimpressed and Sir Stafford Cripps, Lord Privy Seal and Leader of the House of Commons, was sufficiently enthusiastic to agree that the matter should be studied in more detail.

Habbakuk would have to be built in a place where the temperature was below freezing for a long enough period of year. Canada immediately came to mind and the action moved to North America. The services of the Brooklyn Polytechnic, New York, were enlisted for some of the more academic studies and the Universities of Manitoba and Saskatchewan were also involved. But the greater part of the burden fell on Dr C. J. Mackenzie, President of the National Research Council of Canada. Dr Mackenzie was charged with overseeing the construction of a giant model of the proposed *Habbakuk*. To assist him, he enlisted a Montreal engineering company that specialized in refrigeration.

Afterwards, Dr Mackenzie recalled that a 'project, conceived in the boldest manner and on a grand scale in every way, occupied my personal attention most of my waking hours for four feverish months.' Perhaps 'feverish' was not quite the right adjective, for the work was carried out in temperatures that sometimes fell to 40 degrees below zero. But it was nonetheless evocative.

According to the official press release, a team of fifteen men were employed on the project (another source says fifty). Working on the frozen surface of Lake Patricia, it took them about two months to construct a Pykrete iceberg 60 feet long, 30 feet wide, 20 feet deep, and weighing about 1,000 tons. A one horse power engine sufficed to power the refrigerating plant. On the face of it, the experiment seemed to be successful. When the ice of Lake Patricia melted, it remained afloat and it was still to be seen, undiminished, in the winter of 1944. But, by then, it had become an object of no importance.

Pyke had estimated that no more steel would be needed for his two-million-ton masterpiece than that required to build a destroyer. There would, of course, have to be a number of girders (wood was used in the Lake Patricia venture): there would have to be rudders, screws, engines, and driving shafts – that was about all. As he took pains to point out, the method of propulsion was another revolutionary feature. Thirteen screws would be situated on each side of the hull, and each contained in a nacelle, or outer casing, similar to that which houses an aircraft's engine. Thus two or three or four could be put out of action by a torpedo and the ship (if that is the right word) would still be navigable.

What he seems to have overlooked is the fact that the hull would need an insulating skin to keep the Pykrete permanently cold. That would require raw materials beyond the scope of nature, and what would happen if a torpedo pierced *that*?

Despite the impressive achievement of those workers on Lake Patricia, the task of building *Habbakuk* would be a slow and costly business (estimates rose steadily from 'a few thousand pounds' that tripped off Mountbatten's tongue, to £6 million to £8 million, until it reached a staggering £17 million). Inevitably, somebody asked, if it was going to take all that much money and trouble, why not build a normal aircraft carrier? It might be quicker and cheaper in the long run.

There was also the problem of where to build it. A sub-zero temperature (despite a rather optimistic view that it could be constructed in a cold store) was one prerequisite. Another was that whatever site was chosen should be accessible to the sea. This, when one considers the proposed vessel's immense draught, was asking rather a lot. For reasons that have never been convincingly revealed, but which are not difficult to guess, Russia was ruled out. Alaska was eliminated as too remote, and, farther south, the waters of Puget Sound off Seattle were considered to be too warm. Over in the east, the Saguenay River, which debouches into the Saint Lawrence was considered a possibility – until somebody pointed out that a bar of sand at the mouth would block the exit. Corner Brook in Newfoundland and Seven Islands Bay in Quebec were also considered. Neither quite came up to the qualifications that insisted on large pulp factories in the vicinity and the ability to provide a considerable labour force.

But, by this time, the need for *Habbakuk* had largely disappeared. The introduction of centrimetric radar by the Allied navies had made U-boats very much easier to detect and, consequently, to destroy. Long-range tanks fitted to fighters, and the acquisition of bases in the Azores, had done much to reduce the perils of the so-called 'Black Pit' – that perilous stretch of the North Atlantic into which convoys had steamed without any air cover. Furthermore, the Chiefs of Staff had now decided upon a plan for the invasion of Europe. There would be no need for 'floating islands' to assist the deployment of aircraft. The mainland of Britain would do perfectly well.

So far as the war in Europe was concerned, the need for *Habbakuk* had gone. The United States were offered the ideas for the prosecution of the war against Japan. But the US Navy, sceptical from the start, uttered a polite 'thank you' and rejected the proposal.

Poor Pyke! He had cherished such grand dreams – even to Pykrete merchant ships sailing in convoys with neon signs on their decks saying 'Bomb me – I'm a dummy'. Nor was this the end of it. Before the war was very much older, he was to hear of another apparently crazy idea that was adopted and which did work. Indeed, without it, the Allied landings in Normandy might never have been possible. It was called 'Mulberry' harbour.

However, his restless spirit of invention was not yet exhausted. VE Day might have seen the end of war in Europe, but the Japanese had yet to be conquered. This, inevitably, would mean putting men ashore at one place or another. Why, Mr Pyke wondered, bother with landing-craft? He had a much better idea. Pneumatic tubes, each three feet in diameter, could be arranged to link ships with shores. Men and, provided they were small enough, stores could be shot through them at considerable speed. There were no takers.

Geoffrey Pyke may have been a genius: he was also a figure of tragedy. One evening in 1948, he shaved off his beard, took a rather large dose of sleeping tablets and sat down to write his last words. As the drugs took effect, his handwriting degenerated into a scrawl and then the scrawl stopped. The man who dreamed such fantastic dreams, the intellectual whose arrogance suggested such supreme self-confidence, was dead.

Did he feel that the postwar world offered no opportunities for eccentrics such as he (though he would never have admitted that he was one)? Did he have bitter memories of the 'twenties and 'thirties, when his brilliance passed without recognition and his lot was poverty? Was it all too much? Possibly. The only memorials to his achievements had been the 'Weasel' and that strange object on a remote Canadian Lake. But *Habbakuk* –or, rather, what should have been its foetus – had long melted away. Neither Pyke nor Pykrete could endure the rigours of time.